On a cloudy

Silver Linings

Dayle Allen Shockley

Pacific Press Publishing Association
Nampa, Idaho
Oshawa, Ontario, Canada

Edited by Kenneth R. Wade
Stained-glass art by Michael C. Booth
Designed by Dennis Ferree

Copyright ©1997 by
Pacific Press Publishing Association
Printed in the United States of America
All Rights Reserved

Shockley, Dayle Allen, 1955-
    Silver linings : on a cloudy day look for / Dayle
Allen Shockley.
      p.   cm.
    ISBN 0-8163-1371-7 (pbk. : alk. paper)
    1. Meditations.   I. Title.
BV4811.S378 1997
242—dc20   96-36052
                                  CIP

97 98 99 00 01 • 5 4 3 2 1

Table of Contents

Dedication

To my loyal husband, Stan,
whom I love so much.
We're proof that *true love*
can weather any storm.

Acknowledgments

y heartfelt gratitude:

To Almighty God for answering my prayers and opening doors this past year; doors I had knocked on for so long.

To Charles Reel and Jerry Thomas, and the entire trade team at Pacific Press, for asking me to write another "stained-glass cover" book, and for believing I could.

To Mother and Daddy, Elaine, Gayle, David, Charles, Shelaine, and Leslie for their undying love and support. I am so blessed.

To my wonderful daughter Anna for her patience during the many hours I spent on this project. You, Anna Marie Shockley, are my flower from the Lord.

To those who allowed me to share their stories. The power of the pen has eternal effects.

And to all you kind folks who asked, "When is your next book coming out?" Here it is. Thank you for buying it, and I hope it inspires you to look for your own "silver linings."

Treasure each other in the recognition that we do not know how long we shall have each other.
Joshua Loth Liebman

The Shoes

As I walked through the dimly lit house one evening, I stumbled across my husband's size-13 black tennis shoes. I went crashing to the floor, taking with me several picture frames from the coffee table.

Why can't he put his shoes in the closet? I asked myself. He knows I hate tripping over them.

Just then my husband yelled from the back of the house, "What's all the racket about? Are you OK?"

That did it. "No, I'm *not* OK!" I hollered. "Not OK at all!"

Stan came to the door and stared down at me. I could tell he wanted to laugh. "What happened?" he asked, innocently.

"Why can't you just put your stupid shoes in the closet, like normal people?" I grumbled, sitting up to inspect my wounds.

"It might help if you'd turn a light on instead of wandering through the house in the dark," Stan said, smugly.

"That's beside the point, Stan. You know I've asked you

dozens of times to stop leaving your shoes all over the house; they're like two sailboats."

We stared silently at each other across the floor.

"You don't put *my* shoes in the closet," I said, unwilling to get on with my life. "So why should I have to put yours away?"

Saying nothing, he reached for the shoes and disappeared down the hall. I knew they'd be back. It was only a matter of time.

Later in the week, I arrived home and discovered *five* pairs of Stan's shoes in the living room. His house shoes camped under the edge of the couch, his work shoes decorated the hearth, his brown dress shoes jutted out from under the coffee table, his high-tops lay in front of the rocker, and those abominable black tennis shoes glared at me in front of the grandfather clock.

Scowling at the slew of shoes, I had a most malicious and anti-Christian idea. Starting at one end of the living room, I placed all ten shoes in a straight line until they reached the hallway. Breathing hard, I stood back and admired my work. Nobody would be able to get through the room without having to walk over them—or move them.

That'll serve him right, I said to myself. *Let him see what it's like to maneuver around these boats. Better yet, let him see what it's like to have to put them all in the shoe rack.*

I waited for his arrival with much anticipation, but to my dismay, the parade of shoes didn't seem to faze my husband. "What's this?" was all he said. The next time I looked, the shoes were gone. Still, I knew they'd be back. They *always* came back.

One day after driving Anna to school, I returned home, made myself a cup of cocoa, and settled on the couch for a time of devotion. I would try to ignore the familiar size-13 shoes scattered all over the room, but it was difficult. As I read from 1 Thessalonians, I laughed out loud when my eyes came to rest on this verse: "Rejoice evermore" (5:16).

"God," I said, wearily, "If you can give me one good reason to rejoice over these shoes, I'll be happy to do so."

Early next morning I drove my husband to the airport. He was flying to Baltimore for the weekend to participate in the Houston firefighters' annual muscular dystrophy softball tournament. "Have a good time," I said, giving him a kiss at the gate. "See you Monday." He waved me off.

I returned home late in the afternoon, switched on the radio, and started preparing dinner. Suddenly, I heard the announcer's voice saying, "Once again, there are no survivors in that plane crash."

For a moment, my heart stopped. I sat down at the kitchen table, my hands shaking. *Plane crash? What plane crash? Oh, God, no! What plane crash?* But the news was over. Fumbling frantically with the dial, I found another station and heard the tragic details: USAir flight 427 from Chicago to Pittsburgh had gone down, killing all passengers on board.

Shocked by the news, I laid my head on the cold table

and sobbed, both from relief and sadness. Even though my husband was not on that plane, I realized how uncertain life is, and how numbing the shock must be for those families who had loved ones aboard.

That evening, after putting Anna to bed, I stooped to remove Stan's black tennis shoes from where he'd left them in front of the full-length mirror. But instead of putting them away, I put them on. They felt awkward and massive on my small feet.

For several minutes I stood studying my ridiculous reflection in the mirror. Then I looked down at the shoes. They were molded in the exact shape of my husband's feet. I knew every hump and bump so well.

No one could wear these shoes but Stan, I thought to myself. *How would I feel if I knew my husband would never again fill these shoes?* The thought was unthinkable. Somewhere tonight, a woman, without warning, was a widow. Her husband would never again wear his shoes. A chill sliced through my heart. I mourned for her.

The day Stan came home, Anna and I gathered in the living room listening to all the details of his trip; of how his team had gone undefeated in their division. And while Anna admired the shiny, first-place trophy Stan pulled proudly from his bag, I couldn't keep my eyes off the size-13 shoes he'd dropped underneath the coffee table. Funny, I didn't wish them to be anywhere else. They were a comforting sign. My husband was home.

> **"So teach us to number our days. . . ."**
> Psalms 90:12 (KJV)

The Shoes

God of mercy, our days on earth are brief. Sometimes it takes the misfortune of others for us to realize that even the little irritations of life are to be cherished.

Miracles in the Making

I can't remember a time when I didn't want the Singer. I grew up with it. Many were the nights I listened to the whir of this handed-down sewing machine as Mama's hands guided exquisite fabrics across it. And seldom did a day go by that its hum didn't fill the house.

For hours Mama could be found hunched over the Singer, busying herself with cotton prints and small buttons; with satin ribbons and yards of lace. She whipped out dresses fit for a princess to wear. Nothing proved too difficult when it came to her three little girls.

Mama was not one for homemade-looking clothes or a mere "this-will-do" outfit either. She had imagination and energy; lots of energy. There were sailor dresses; dresses with ruffles and petticoats; jewel necklines; Peter Pan collars; and wide, velvet sashes.

She also possessed a flare for the unusual, for embroidered pockets, for appliqued collars, for exotic border prints.

It was not unusual for Mama to carry pen and paper to the expensive department stores. Contemplatively, she studied the complex outfits hanging in the window, tilting her head this way and that, drinking in the full view.

By the time we arrived home, Mama had a sketchy drawing, remarkably like the costly dress in the window. With grim determination splashed across her face, she carefully set out to fashion a dress of equal beauty and resplendence, often making her own pattern from an old newspaper.

Excellence was Mama's goal. She spent a lot of time measuring and marking, gathering and stitching, slowly bringing her creation to perfection.

Before long, Mama's voice would call to me. Time for a fitting. I can still remember standing under her serious stare, inhaling the virgin cloth, her skillful hands tucking and pinning.

Mama's sewing ability appeared endless. Not only were we kids dressed flawlessly, so were our dolls. One Christmas, my twin sister and I received identical wardrobes for our ten-inch fashion dolls.

Created by my mother's clever hands, each tiny piece appeared magnificently stitched, a mirror of their creator's vivid imagination. There was a royal blue formal gown, high-waisted, complete with silver sequins and white net; a flannel housecoat, buttoning down the front; a bright red shift dress, with a ruffle along the tail. There was even a girdle! My mouth gaped as I stared in wonder at the dainty garments nestled inside the white tissue. I was convinced Mama and the Singer could work miracles.

I remember the night, several years ago, when Mama

called. The Singer was not being used (she had finally bought a new one). Would I be interested in baby-sitting it for a while? Would I!

When the machine arrived, a few days later, I felt downright weepy as I steadied it in front of the spare bedroom window, resisting the urge to hug it. I couldn't wait to hear its steady hum fill my home.

Not long ago, I stood in front of my little daughter, a batch of pins hanging from my lips. Hesitantly, I wrapped my humble creation around her small body, the fabric's pure scent rising to meet me. As I critically studied the simple cotton dress, I felt discouraged. "Well, it sure can't compare to anything of Nana's," I said.

Stiffly, Anna patted my arm, carefully dodging the pins I wielded. "But Mama," she said, sweetly. "Even Nana had to start *somewhere*."

And so she did, as do we all.

"Whatever your hand finds to do,
do it with all your might."
Ecclesiastes 9:10 (NIV)

Lord, help me view my humble beginnings
as the first step toward victory.

*When God is going to do something wonderful, He begins
with a difficulty; if He is going to do something very
wonderful, He begins with an impossibility.*
Anonymous

Something From Nothing

e were crazy in love. Texas was green,
and summer lay across the fields in shades of red, orange,
and yellow. We'd been married only three years, and even
though money was tight, Stan and I believed love would
conquer all.

But that was before the car broke down. Not the car that
had quit running two months earlier, but the one we'd been
sharing until we could afford to get the other one repaired.
Now, they both sat silent in the driveway, hoods up, like
opened mouths screaming for cash.

It couldn't have come at a worse time. It was ten days
before payday, and two weeks earlier Stan had made a pledge
for an outreach project at church. He promised to give
$1,000 by the end of August, a mere three months away. It
had seemed like an outrageous pledge, but I was proud of
my husband for wanting to give to this worthy cause. We
figured with enough scrimping between us, we could do it.
I wasn't so sure anymore.

Through the screen door, I looked at Stan draped across the engine of the green Thunderbird, an anxious look on his face. It seemed our married life had consisted of one calamity after another. Practically every other week, something either stopped working or started making peculiar noises, keeping us grinding our teeth at night. Despair surrounded me like a wet blanket, and I did not have the energy to stop it.

Moving to the piano, I sat down to play. Many had been the times I played away my blues. But not today. There was no music in my hands. Every chord rang bleak and lifeless, an elegy of doom.

"Oh, Lord," I whispered, "You see the need. You're our only hope."

Stan appeared in the doorway, the strain of our predicament engraved on his face. He wiped his brow with the back of his hand. "I guess I'm gonna have to take it somewhere," he announced, rubbing grimy fingers on an old rag before picking up the telephone.

My spirit sank lower as I listened while he discussed motors and thermostats with someone we'd never met. And I felt faint when he hung up and announced, "It's gonna cost about three-hundred dollars to fix it."

It may as well have been three million. "How," I begged, "are we ever going to come up with that?"

Stan shrugged. "Take it out of the checking account, I guess."

"But I haven't paid any bills yet, and we haven't bought groceries, and . . ."

"Dayle," he said, bluntly. "We have to have a car. That

other stuff will just have to wait."

"What about the savings account?" It was a new account Stan contributed to bi-weekly. I knew there wasn't much money in it yet, but maybe it would cover the car's expense.

"No," he said, shaking his head fiercely. "That's for retirement. Besides, it would barely cover what we need."

"Well, you'll never retire if you can't get to work," I said, on the verge of tears.

"Hey," Stan said, placing a finger under my chin. "It'll be all right. We're gonna make it." He sounded so sure. "Quit worrying."

By Friday evening, the Thunderbird hummed agreeably in the driveway. I had contacted the creditors, who graciously offered fifteen days of grace. That left one problem. The food supply was dwindling, and payday was still nine days away. Stan seemed undaunted by this fact, constantly admonishing me to, "Quit worrying," as if he knew something I didn't.

On Monday, I took inspection of the kitchen. Outside of a clutter of condiments, the refrigerator housed a wilted head of lettuce, a bowl of leftover corn, two eggs, and a soda with no fizz. Inside the freezer was a small package containing a leftover entree and a bag of frozen broccoli. The pantry held a lonely box of popping corn. We could probably make it nine more days, I reasoned, but it sure wouldn't be fun, nor tasty.

There were a host of friends who would have come to our rescue, had they known our plight; our parents would have insisted on wiring us money; I even had a sister living in the same town. But I couldn't imagine telling anyone I needed food. I had *never* needed food. In my mind, this resembled something right out of the Great Depression, not 1983. I felt sick.

Trudging into the bedroom, I fell to my knees beside the bed, mentally exhausted. I rested my head against the cool satin coverlet and stared out the window. And then, big tears rolled across the bridge of my nose, soaking the side of my face. I didn't try to stop them. I thought about praying, but I couldn't seem to form the words, so I just cried quietly.

My Bible lay on the night stand. I'd heard about people flopping open their Bibles, and boom, there was the exact verse they needed. It wasn't my style, but, taking a giant leap of faith, I opened my Bible. It opened to Job 26. Verse 7 leapt out at me: "He stretcheth the north over the empty place, and hangeth the earth upon nothing."

Grabbing a pen, I underlined the verse. "If you hung the earth on nothing, Lord," I said, assuredly, "You can do *anything*, including keeping us from going hungry."

I stood up, dried my face, and jumped sky high when a knock sounded at the front door. *Who on earth is that?* I wondered.

Flinging open the door, there stood my sister, Elaine, smiling her beautiful smile. "Hi!" she said, cheerily. "I thought you might need some groceries, so I brought you some."

I must have looked like I'd seen a ghost. Circled around her sat five grocery bags. I could not believe my eyes. Splendid items like fresh vegetables, bread, pretzels, and cookies, and a two-liter soda bottle hung over the top of the sacks. I turned aside, hoping she hadn't seen the tears threatening to slide down my face.

Elaine knew money had been tight in recent months, she knew about the pledge, but she could not have known about the car, nor the empty pantry.

"Elaine!" I hollered. "Why did you do this? You shouldn't have." She fixed her jaw real hard. " 'Cause I felt like it." She hugged me tight. "Now, I can't stay, so help me grab these bags."

I never did tell Elaine just how barren the kitchen had been that day, and how angelic she looked standing on the porch, the sun on her face. I never told anyone. Maybe that makes me a coward. I don't know.

I do know when August rolled around, we paid our thousand-dollar pledge. I also know that lonely box of popping corn is still with me. It has survived three moves and more than a dozen years. I keep it as a monument to God's awesome power.

"Is anything too hard for the Lord?"
Genesis 18:14, (KJV)
Dear God, when the cupboard is bare,
I'm not afraid.
You're a pro at making stuff from scratch.

God will not permit any troubles to come upon us unless He has a specific place by which great blessing can come out of the difficulty.
Peter Marshall

Life After Death

orning lay over the land in a misty gray fog as Rita Banks* crawled out of bed and stumbled to the bathroom. Her head throbbed, as it did most every morning. Glaring at her haggard reflection in the mirror, Rita reached for the half-empty bottle of wine on the counter, tilted back her head, and drank every drop. *Ah!* she thought, *maybe now I can face the day.*

The house was hushed as she walked through, stopping outside her son's bedroom door. Ten weeks had passed since the accident, yet the room remained just as her twelve-year-old left it his last day alive. Rich had made his bed that morning. Rita wasn't surprised, though. He'd helped out around the house a lot after he started attending church with a neighbor boy. She had been proud of her son and wished she had the courage to make changes in her own life.

As tears gathered in her eyes, Rita moved to Rich's desk and eased into his chair. It was the first time she'd sat down in her son's room since his death. Feelings of guilt surged through her as she remembered past years.

Rita knew her drinking had bothered Rich, but he seldom brought up the subject. Even at the young age of twelve, he seemed equipped with the necessary skills for surviving life's blows. Every morning, without complaint, he got himself off to school; he knew his mom wouldn't wake up. He fixed his breakfast, prepared his lunch, and walked to the corner to catch the bus. Most afternoons, he'd find Rita passed out on the couch, an empty liquor bottle on the coffee table. Rita often wondered how he managed. Inwardly, she longed to be like Rich. He seemed so strong and able to cope with the daily grind of living.

Rita had never been strong. Even at the age of eighteen, when she married Rob, she leaned heavily on alcohol to pull her through heartaches and hardships. Two years later, Rich had been born. Through the years, Rita had tried to quit drinking. She'd joined every conceivable program, but after a few months of sobriety, she turned back to the bottle. Finally, four years ago, Rob split, leaving her to raise their son. And now Rich was dead.

Laying across the little desk, Rita sobbed, "Oh, Rich, I hope you knew how very much I loved you, son. I hope you knew how much I wanted to quit drinking. I really do want to quit, son." She sat up and looked intently at her son's seventh-grade picture. He was smiling that lopsided smile of his, hoping to hide his crooked teeth. Rita ached to hear his voice one more time, to wrap her arms around him one more time, to take him to the zoo one more time. "Please speak to me, Richard," she said, her voice pleading. "Please, Rich."

With trembling hands, she opened the desk's drawers and began sorting through her son's things. There was a folder labeled "Art," which held an assortment of pencil sketches, some Rita recognized, others she'd never seen. She'd have them matted and framed one day, she decided. Another folder contained book reports he'd written.

Just as she was about to close the drawer, Rita's heart skipped a beat. Stuffed in a far corner was a small yellow envelope. On the outside was one word: "Mom."

Hardly breathing, she slit the seal and drew out a folded sheet of notebook paper. Dated two days before the accident, the letter read:

Dear Mom:

I'm really sorry you felt bad last night and couldn't come to my basketball game. We lost, but I scored six points. Maybe you can come next time. I hope you won't be mad at me for saying this, but I sure wish you would stop drinking so much. I know it hurt you when Daddy left, but you still have me, and I love you very much. When you are sober, you are a very nice lady. I hate to see you wasting your life like this. Drinking is not making your problems go away. It only makes you go away. When you have had too much to drink, you sort of like disappear. I hope you know I really love you even if I don't say it much. Would you like to go to church with me and Dave sometime?

Love, Rich

Rita felt as if her son stood there, reading the letter to her; she could almost hear his voice. Overcome with grief, she threw herself across Rich's bed and fell into a troubled sleep.

When she awoke, she stumbled into the kitchen, still clutching her son's letter, and opened the cabinets. Four bottles of liquor stared back at her, but instead of wanting them, Rita was surprised to find them unappealing. She had never refused a drink. Pulling the bottles off the shelf, Rita calmly unscrewed the caps and poured the contents into the kitchen sink.

That was four years ago. Miraculously, Rita has never had another drink. In fact, Rita says her life today is nothing short of a miracle. At thirty-six, she feels like a teenager again. She's remarried and has a new baby. And on weekends, she and her family can be found worshiping.

"I know it sounds ridiculous," Rita says, "but Rich's letter probably wouldn't have been effective had he still been alive; I probably would still be a hopeless alcoholic. But I believe God allowed his letter to come to me from the grave. God knew it was the only way I would have ever surrendered to Him."

By giving up the bottle, Rita hopes it, in some way, repays Rich for all the times she wasn't there for him.

"I guess you could say that it took Rich's death for me to get back my life. I know Rich is in God's care now," says Rita. "And one day, we'll be together again."

"Him that overcometh will I make a pillar in the temple of my God. . . ."
Revelation 3:12 (KJV)

Precious Lord, how often have we stood
at the grave of a family member or friend
and vowed to "turn over a new leaf"
on their behalf. But daily tasks
have a way of fading our memories.
Please give us the fortitude to put action
behind our words.

* Not her real name.

Take time to laugh—
it is the music of the soul.
Anonymous

Gains and Losses

y flight out of New Orleans was scheduled for departure at 1:20 in the afternoon. Anna was barely three months old. She and I had enjoyed a few precious days with my parents in Mississippi. Now I sat in the back seat of the car, wondering if we were going to make it to the airport in time.

Even though my parents live a hundred miles from New Orleans, we'd allowed plenty of travel time. But due to some problems with a tire, we'd made a couple of unexpected stops. It looked as if I might miss my flight.

It was nearing one o'clock when we arrived at the airport. Had I been a lone traveler, things could have moved more smoothly, but traveling with a baby tends to slow you down. Not only do you have to tote the baby, you have to lug a host of assorted items—diaper bag, infant seat, stroller. Heavy stuff.

Realizing that time was of the essence, Daddy let me out at the door. I charged into the terminal, Anna in my arms, and ran to the ticket counter, while my mother ran behind me, pushing Anna's stroller and carrying my briefcase.

At the ticket counter, to my horror, the young woman could not locate my ticket. Near tears, I pled with her to please hurry, but she seemed oblivious to my plight, insisting the mix up was my fault instead of her own.

Finally, at 1:15, she "found" the ticket and directed us to our gate. Like a wild mustang, I dashed down the long corridor, weaving in and out of throngs of people, Anna's head bobbing against my chest, while Mother and the stroller chased after us.

When we reached the gate, I was gasping for air. A young man behind the counter took my ticket and sadly shook his head. The plane had already taxied down the runway and was about to take off. There was no choice but to take a later flight.

I teetered on that delicate rim between sensible and senseless. It had not been a prosperous morning. Falling into the nearest chair to catch my breath, it dawned on me that Anna had not made a sound since I sprinted from the ticket counter. For a split second, I wondered if I had squeezed her unconscious while running through the terminal.

Glancing down at her, I was shocked. Anna lay in my arms, grinning from ear to ear. The expression on her face clearly said, "That was fun, Mama; can we run some more?"

Despite the tears of frustration in my eyes, the sight of her smiling face sent me into a fit of laughing. And when I told Mother to look at Anna's face, we became hysterical. So while we cackled like a couple of hens, the young man behind the check-in counter stared at us as if we'd fallen off the turnip truck. I'm sure he'd never seen anyone get that thrilled over missing a flight.

I soon realized the day had not been a total loss. Why, I felt better than I'd felt in weeks. And all because I'd had a good laugh.

"A merry heart doeth good, like a medicine."
Proverbs 17:22 (KJV)

**When the day seems a total washout, Lord,
thank You for the cleansing effect of laughter.**

The man who removes a mountain
begins by carrying away small stones.
Chinese Proverb

Step by Step

On a sweltering day in July, I stood slumped over a wobbly ladder in the backyard, sweat trickling down my face and neck. It had to be ninety-five degrees. Straightening up, I surveyed the section of paint I'd just applied to the side of the garage, and assessed how much more there was to be done. Mind blowing! I let out a horrific moan and climbed down. My husband stood a few feet away, deep in trim work.

For the most part, my husband and I are sane people. However, there are those times when we make decisions that leave us both shaking our heads.

The decision to paint the exterior of our house did not come easy. For two years we toyed with the idea, counting the cost—both on our bodies and pocketbook. Finally, we took the plunge, and, at times, we did indeed shake our heads, wondering if we'd bitten off more than we could chew. To make matters worse, the only time we had ample opportunity to paint was during the height of Houston's boiling summer.

"I've just got to get out of this heat for a while," I told my husband. "I'm about to have a stroke." He grunted a reply. "I'll make us some iced tea and sandwiches," I offered.

When I got to the kitchen, the phone was ringing.

"Hello," I said, out of breath.

The woman's voice on the other end quivered. A pathetic sound, like a wounded animal. It was a friend I'd not heard from in a spell, and for the next hour I listened as she spilled the whole sordid details.

Her husband, an upstanding man among friends and community, was involved with another woman. Not just another woman, but her best friend.

Finally, through deep sobs, she asked, "Dayle, how am I going to get through this? I miss him so much!"

Of course, I tried to say all the right words to this broken woman. I assured her that nothing was too hard for the Lord, that He would be a pillar of strength during this difficult time. I reminded her of the people she knew who had survived similar tragedies, that if they could do it, so could she. I quoted Scripture to her. I prayed with her. But, in the end, I told her how pitifully inadequate my words seemed. Not that I doubt God's Word; not that I don't believe in prayer, but, like it or not, sometimes life sends us vicious blows that leave us paralyzed, unable to believe it, let alone understand it. This was a perfect example. I wished so badly for a magic wand.

The phone call haunted me the rest of the day. As I worked, I thought of how sad it was to see not one, but two families torn asunder. Pointing fingers resulted in nothing.

It was too late. Lives would be forever scarred because of self-centered desires.

Early next morning, I walked outside and watched a fiery sun appear over the treetops in the backyard. It promised to be another scorcher. As I rounded the side of the garage, my feet and hands aching from weeks of painting and standing, I was taken aback at just how far I'd painted yesterday. With a little luck, the garage would be done by noon.

Funny, I thought, *yesterday the job seemed more than I could handle. Today, a simple task.*

I thought of my hurting friend, and I breathed a prayer for her. I would phone her later, and reveal to her an old truth I'd just again realized: Looking at the "big picture" can be oppressive, overwhelming. The only way to get through *anything*—whether it's as trivial as painting a house, or as grievous as surviving a mate's infidelity—is one step at a time. And it is only by God's strength that we are able to pick up our feet and inch forward.

With renewed vigor, I climbed onto the shaky ladder and dipped my brush into the creamy tan paint.

"God is our refuge and strength,
a very present help in trouble."
Psalm 46:1 (KJV)

Lord, when the task before me
seems an impossibility, help me understand that,
without Your strength, it is.
Only by clinging to You, can I survive.

What really counts is what you learn
after you know it all.
Anonymous

Mercy

turned twenty-two the year I bought the white corvette, a splendid, low car with mag wheels and T-tops—a beautiful machine with a powerful hum and a maximum speed of 160—sleek and full of fire.

Racy and raring to fly off at the slightest provocation, the car and I had much in common. Perched behind its wheel, I felt certain there was little I had left to learn about life. That's when Mr. Smith came to manage the branch office where I worked as a customer representative.

Mr. Smith, a quiet man with black-rimmed glasses, had a face that always smiled. He moved in a polished way, smoothly, as if certain he was headed in the right direction. Yet he possessed a particular naivete, blushing freely, cackling at knock-knock jokes.

One Monday morning my immediate supervisor, whom I'll call Mr. Jones, announced a meeting. It was no secret that I disliked Mr. Jones; the feeling was mutual. On more than one occasion, he and I had clashed, sending sparks flying like two live wires in a rainstorm. So, not a little irritated, I drifted into the meeting and took a chair. Lunch was a half hour away, I had a date and was starving already.

As soon as the meeting began, I sensed something was askew. Mr. Jones had already begun sweating—something he did under duress—and the room reeked of unpleasant odors. I sat quietly, inspecting my perfectly groomed nails, trying hard not to breathe.

About midway through the meeting, Mr. Jones became visibly upset, swearing and cursing. After he used God's name a couple of times, I flew out of my chair, announced, "I don't have to listen to that kind of language," and stomped noisily out of the room, leaving Mr. Jones and all of my co-workers staring after me in stunned disbelief.

Promptly, Mr. Jones chased after me, ordering me into Mr. Smith's office. Once there, I collapsed into the nearest chair and burst into tears.

With a wave of his hand, Mr. Smith dismissed the flustered Mr. Jones and sat there silently while I attempted to compose myself. For several minutes, I blubbered and sobbed, trying desperately to excuse my irrational behavior.

Still, Mr. Smith said nothing, reached inside his navy blazer, handed me a crisp, white handkerchief, motioned for me to use it. Then, calmly, he asked, "What happened out there?"

"I don't know," I said between sobs. "*He* started cussing and I guess I just lost my temper. Sometimes that man makes me *so mad!*" I was yelling.

"Maybe so, Dayle, but he is your boss. You must show

him respect." As always, Mr. Smith was smiling.

Just then, a faint knock sounded at the door. Mr. Jones peeked inside, his face beet red. "When you get through in here," he said, glaring at me, "come back to the meeting; you need to hear what we're discussing."

And that's when, unable to stop my silly, impetuous self, I leapt up out of the chair and roared, "I am *not* coming back to your stupid meeting!"

"Dayle," Mr. Smith pleaded futilely in the background, "Please! *Sit down.*"

But I would not. Fuming, I charged past Mr. Jones, headed straight for my desk, snatched my purse, and plunged out the door trembling, while my co-workers sat like statues, watching this astonishing scene unfold.

"Where are you going?" Mr. Smith, now standing in the center of the room, called after me.

"I don't know!" I hollered, loud enough for the entire tenth floor to hear.

In the elevator, I dabbed at my eyes with Mr. Smith's wilted handkerchief, wondering what on earth I had just done. How ignorant and undisciplined could I be? I had a good job with a major corporation. Now what did I have? Without question, a tarnished job history and a white Corvette would not escort me far in life. Still—it was too late to do anything about it. For how could I return after such a dramatic exit?

Lunch proved disastrous. My friend kept asking what was bothering me; I kept saying, "Nothing," but I couldn't complete a sentence without tears. Finally, I spilled the entire story, ending with, "What am I going to do?"

"You're going back and talk to your boss—if you want to keep your job," my wise friend said.

My stomach in knots, I returned to the building, walked to the house phone, and punched the number. When Mr. Smith came on the line, I said simply, "This is Dayle."

"Yes, Dayle, what is it?"

"Mr. Smith," I began, feebly. "I'm really sorry about what happened. Could we—I mean—I was just wondering—do you reckon—Could we talk?"

"Where are you?"

"I'm downstairs in the lobby."

"I'll be right down."

Five minutes later, Mr. Smith emerged from the elevator, strode evenly toward me and—unbelievably—smiled. "Why don't we go for a ride in my car," he suggested, his voice strained. Together, we strolled out of the building into the steamy Texas sunshine, a sense of urgency looming between us. I wondered if he would fire me. He had every right.

It was sweltering in the car. No one spoke. Sitting there like two stones, we ambled out into the street, the air conditioner pumping hot air. We rode two blocks and stopped next to a low-income apartment complex. Aluminum foil squares clung to the windows like tiny shields against the Texas heat.

Drawing his breath in sharply, Mr. Smith said, "Dayle, I must say, I am disappointed in you."

Staring dumbly out my window, I felt about an inch high.

"You know I could fire you for insubordination."

"I know," I said, barely above a whisper. "You should."

He sighed long and hard. "Maybe," he said. "But I'm

not going to."

Slowly I turned toward him, hoping I'd heard correctly. "You're . . . not?"

"No. I'm not," he said flatly. "You're a hard worker, and I know you're a good person. I also know you're young. There's a lot to learn about getting along with people, and it takes time. That's why I want to give you a second chance." A second chance? He was offering me a second chance? My heart leapt inside of me. I didn't know what to say. Yet there was so much I wanted to say.

We rode in awkward silence to the parking lot and got out.

"Well," Mr. Smith said, smiling, "I hope you've learned a lesson through all this, Dayle. Now, why don't you take the rest of the day off, go home, get some rest, and I'll see you in the morning."

Dumbfounded, I mumbled my thanks, watched him disappear into the building, and drove off, the Corvette at a slow pace.

In retrospect, what could have been a devastating event for me—though duly deserved—turned into a wake-up call. That day marked the dawning of maturity; the beginning of tolerance. My youth had been a breeding ground for self-centeredness, impatience, an unforgiving spirit. But because of Mr. Smith, I learned a most important lesson: It is a good thing to show mercy; one never knows when one might need it.

"Blessed are the merciful: for they shall obtain mercy."
Matthew 5:7 (KJV)

Dear Lord, it isn't always easy showing mercy,
offering second chances, forgiving human errors.
Help me understand that in doing so,
I make myself a recipient of the same.

Remember this—
that very little is needed to make a happy life.
Marcus Aurelius

Keepsakes for a Lifetime

was only twelve when Maw Maw died. Maw Maw was my paternal grandmother, a tall, plain woman with a kind face and a mass of long white hair.

To the distant spectator, Maw Maw possessed very little. She never lived in a fancy house, never drove a fine car. The few furnishings she did own were simple and modest. Yet some of my fondest memories took place at the home of this unassuming woman.

When I was about seven Maw Maw lived in a scanty house in rural Mississippi, no indoor plumbing, an old wood stove, and only the warmth of a fireplace on frigid winter nights.

Maw Maw walked to the well for water every day. Many were the times she took me along with her. Together we'd march through the nippy air, the water pot clanging between us like a church bell. Generally, Maw Maw whistled as we strolled—some easy tune she made up as she went. When the well popped into view, I'd break into a run, the wind beating against my upturned face. Then I'd watch her drop the water pot over the side, hear the low gurgling below, and stare wide-eyed as the bucket surfaced, Maw Maw carefully reeling it up. Homeward we'd trudge, our gait slow and determined.

Over the years, Maw Maw lived in a number of houses; each one a little nicer than the last. I was entranced when she and Paw Paw rented a little green cement block house, with a drafty old barn out back. My sisters and I spent many a glorious afternoon leaping over haystacks, hiding from make-believe enemies. We'd romp until the shadows gathered outside, sending us flying, lickety-split to the back door of the house.

At bedtime, Maw Maw gathered us all around for a time of prayer and hugs and kisses. Then, three sleepy heads would pile into one bed, snuggling between thin flannel blankets. Even now, if I try real hard, I can summon the smell of those blankets around my face. I can remember the wind whistling at the windows, the dampness of the room, and how warm and cozy I felt tucked beneath those fleecy covers.

In the morning, Maw Maw's humming floated through the house as she stood at the kitchen counter rolling out fat homemade biscuits, a cloud of flour about her head. In a little while we gathered around a small table heavy with hot biscuits, fresh eggs, white gravy, and smoking black coffee.

As we settled in, Maw Maw would stroll around the table, patting each one on the back, making sure everyone—except herself—had a place to sit. This gentle woman loved her family with a fiery passion.

On a cold morning in January, Maw Maw drew her final breath. It seems a lifetime ago, yet Maw Maw lives on: In the homemade biscuits I love to create using her "recipe," in the scrap quilt she and my mom pieced together some forty years ago, and in her great-granddaughter—my daughter—who carries her name, Anna.

Maw Maw is proof that wealth is not measured by the size of one's estate at the end of life's journey, but by the splendid memories collected while getting there.

*"A man's life consisteth not in the abundance
of the things which he possesseth."*
Luke 12:15 (KJV)

**Dear Lord, no matter how little I own,
may the memories I leave
be rich in truth and love.**

The force of prayer is greater than any possible combination of man-made or man-controlled powers because prayer is man's greatest means of tapping the infinite resources of God.
J. Edgar Hoover

Forgotten Keys

At 10:30 Friday night my husband and I stood under a full moon, in a deserted parking lot, pointing accusing fingers at each other.

"Why didn't you put your keys in your purse?"

"I thought you had yours in your pocket."

"Well, I don't."

"Why don't you?"

Whatever the reasons, both sets of keys lay on the console—inside our locked van—mocking us.

For a while, Stan puttered around with a pocketknife, poking at the vent window on one side.

"You're not going to get anything open with that," I growled.

"Just be quiet, would you?" he said, stalking around tapping on each window, as if by some magical phenomenon they would open up.

"Why are you doing that?" I asked.

"I've gotten in like this before," he said, although he didn't convince me. Suddenly, he stopped and looked at me. "What have you got in your purse?"

"Nothing."

"You don't have a fingernail file?"

"Yes, but you'd just break it, and we'd still be locked out," I said. "It won't unlock that door."

"What else do you have?"

"Nothing."

"Dayle, you're bound to have *something* in your purse that I can use," he exclaimed, as if I carried slim jims and coat hangers in my wallet.

"I *don't!*" I said, my frustration apparent.

"Well, just look!" he roared.

Muttering, I flung open my bag and pulled out the first thing I saw, a flimsy, gray comb. "Here."

He rolled his eyes. "That's not going to do any good."

"No kidding. Well, I could offer you a fresh tube of lip gloss."

"Dayle, don't you have any old keys or something like that?"

The man would not give up. "No, sweetheart, I don't."

For a while, we stared at each other, a helpless look passing between us. There didn't seem to be an easy solution for this one.

"Wait!" I said. "I've got an extra key to the van! I sure do! I've got another key in my coin purse!" Digging madly inside my purse, I drew out a gleaming silver key and, with sort of a bow, presented it to my husband.

He smiled a roguish grin and said "Why, thank you, madam," and calmly unlocked the door.

On the drive home, I thought of other "locked doors" in my life and in the lives of God's children everywhere: unsaved families, abusive spouses, substance addictions, sickness, affliction, financial calamity. I wondered if somewhere out there accusing fingers were being pointed; thoughts of giving up dominating conversations. I had certainly experienced those times.

And I also realized that I have, in my possession, a key, just waiting to be discovered. The key is called "prayer" and it has never failed to unlock the doors Satan locks. All I have to do is use it.

"If ye shall ask anything in my name, I will do it."
John 14:14 (KJV)

**Father, there are no doors
prayer cannot unlock.
So why, then, don't we pray more often?**

There is more safety with Christ in the tempest than without Christ in the calmest waters.
Alexander Grosse

The Unseen Hand

On a crisp September morning, my father drove me into town for a dental appointment. At seventeen, I still had apprehensions about dental work, dating to early childhood when I once became so frightened I bit my dentist. However, this was going to be a routine filling; nothing to dread. I could not know what lay in store.

With syringe in hand, the dentist poked around in my mouth, searching for the best place to stick me, when he stopped short. "Hmm. What is that?" he asked. "There's a knot right here. Have you noticed it before?"

I shook my head.

The dentist stopped and called for my father. He then asked us to go down the hall and see an oral surgeon, Doctor Black.

Dr. Black, a tall man with a pleasing demeanor, examined every nook and cranny inside my mouth, his fingers coming to rest on The Knot. "You've never noticed this here before?" He seemed curious. "Does it hurt?"

"No, sir."

He washed his hands, folded his arms, and announced, "I'd like to lance that thing today and send it out for a biopsy. I'll call you in a few days with the results."

A few mornings later, Dr. Black gave us the disturbing report, recommending I make an appointment at M. D. Anderson Hospital in Houston for a complete evaluation.

The appointed day arrived. I sat in the Head and Neck Clinic at M. D. Anderson Cancer Research Center in Houston, Texas, not a pretty place to be.

The waiting room was crowded with people of all ages, and I tried to avoid staring at the scenery: people with open cavities where a nose used to be; distorted faces; bald heads.

Suddenly, I heard my name being called. My family shot up like a row of jack-in-the-boxes and trailed the nurse to a tiny room where I sat in a chair in the middle of the floor. Gripping its arms, I glanced at my mom and dad standing across the room. They looked like two pillars of steel.

I was seen by Doctor Oscar Guillamondegui, a bright young doctor whose accent was as confusing as his name. In spite of that, I liked him right off.

Over the next few weeks, my life became consumed by tests and more tests; by blood samples and X-rays. You name it, they did it. But at last, we sat waiting for word from the doctor.

Dr. Guilly (as he is fondly called) got right to the point. "The knot in Dayle's mouth is known as a mucoepidermoid carcinoma, well differentiated, which is a malignant tumor of the minor salivary glands." He recommended immediate surgery and twenty-five rounds of radiation. The prognosis was dependent on the depth of the tumor at the time of surgery.

A heavy silence filled the little room. The only sound was an occasional sniffle from my mother. I felt afraid. My mother reached for my hand, her grip firm. "Everything is going to be OK," that grip seemed to say. "I don't know how, but it will. I just know it will."

Against the doctor's wishes, we did not consent to immediate surgery. All year my family had planned a trip to the mountains in order to attend a religious convention. I begged to go, and I will always be grateful that my parents agreed to make the trip. Maybe God had a special healing for me, a special blessing. At the doctor's insistence, however, surgery was scheduled promptly on my return.

On the last night of the convention, my father arranged for me to be prayed over by the ministers. Nervously, I marched to the front of that mammoth arena, felt hands touch my head, imploring God to heal.

After service, my sister and I were walking with friends to a nearby cafe when I had the strangest sensation. It felt as if The Knot was being squeezed. Eagerly, I reached to see if maybe it had disappeared, but it was still there. Saying nothing to my sister, I wondered if the odd sensation had been only my imagination.

The next morning, my family drove back to Texas, and on Halloween night, I walked into a hospital room decked with black cats, ugly witches, and orange pumpkins. Undaunted by the sight of them, I slipped on a hospital gown and crawled into bed, pulling crisp, white sheets around my face. It would be a long night.

Before daylight, I woke to a great clattering out in the hall. A pretty nurse pushed a metal cart beside my bed and gave me a shot—to calm my nerves. She promised to return for me later. I stared out the window and watched the world wake up. Never had it looked so beautiful.

When the nurse returned with a gurney, I crawled aboard, and we rumbled down a wide hallway, the smell of coffee and scrambled eggs wafting through the corridors. I felt so out of place atop the gurney, like a miserable beached whale. My family walked silently beside me; I sensed their anxiety.

"This is as far as y'all can go," the little nurse announced to my family in a slow Texas drawl.

Her words rattled me.

"Y'all can wait in the waiting area across the hall from the operating room. Dr. Guilly will come out and talk to you after her surgery." Her words sounded memorized, like those of a tour guide.

"Why don't we pray one more time before Dayle goes in," my father said, barely above a whisper. Gathering around, my family joined hands as a prayer went up. When we'd finished, they each kissed me, whispering final words of encouragement. Then, standing in a ragged row, they rendered weak smiles and waved. I waved back.

In a minute, the stretcher rolled forward, plunged through a swinging door, coming to rest in a room filled with patients atop their own gurneys. We looked like airplanes waiting for takeoff.

Hot tears trickled out the corners of my eyes and rolled into my hair. My heart cried out inside of me, afraid of the unknown. But by the time the nurse wheeled me into the operating room, the medication had started working, producing a peculiar, laid-back feeling.

Someone took my hand and said, "Dayle, I'm the anesthesiologist. I'm fixing to give you a little stick. Okay?" She spoke loudly, as if I were hard of hearing.

I turned to see a small, Asian-American woman, with sincere eyes and a smiling face. "This will start your IV," she was saying, pointing to a pole with a bag hanging on it.

I tried to nod.

Watching the IV drip, I wondered if anyone had ever been, accidentally, operated on while still awake.

What a crazy thing to think!

Slowly, the anesthesiologist pushed in the syringe. "What is your doctor's name, Dayle?" Even though she stood at my head, she sounded very far away. I tried to answer her question, but couldn't. Then the room went silent, and I knew nothing.

"Hello, Dayle!" A voice boomed. A hand reached out and patted me. I had heard that voice before, but where?

"This is Dr. Guilly. You did very well in surgery. Everything looks great."

Hours later, I lay in bed listening to a beaming Dr. Guilly describe my surgery. When he got to the tumor, he explained, the roots appeared to have "shriveled up." Because of this, and because of Dr. Guilly's certainty of complete resection, no radiation would be needed.

Even though my jaw stuck out like a grapefruit, I smiled a victorious smile.

Could that have been God's hand that reached inside the

mouth of a frightened seventeen-year-old girl and "shriveled" up the roots of a malignant tumor? I believe it was.

Looking back, I'm grateful for the experience. Not only did it prepare me for future suffering, it taught me that life can be most unkind; there is much heartache, much anguish, even in the lives of Christians. Ah, but the beauty lies in the fact that during the agonizing times of my life, God has been there. His unseen hand will *always* be there, comforting me in my sufferings so that I may comfort a fellow traveler along the way.

> *"Blessed be God . . . the God of all comfort;*
> *who comforteth us in all our tribulation,*
> *that we may be able to comfort them*
> *which are in any trouble, by the comfort*
> *wherewith we ourselves are comforted of God."*
> 2 Corinthians 1:3-4 (KJV)

Gracious God, from my heart, I thank You
for the suffering I have known—and may know—
in this life. Not only has it given my faith roots,
unshakable and unmovable;
it opens my eyes and my arms to other sufferers.

True Love Revealed

nly nine more days," my friend tells me, beaming.

We are hovered around my kitchen table, engaged in a game of Scrabble, when, for the tenth time, she reminds me of her swiftly approaching wedding date.

Frankly, Amy's reminder leaves a bittersweet taste in my mouth. While I've prayed she would find the "perfect" husband, did she have to fall in love with a full-time evangelist who's going to snatch her out of my life, just like that?

Amy's been my bosom buddy for fourteen years. My confidant, my encourager, my prayer partner, my "private-eye" assistant; I can't help but be saddened that she is pulling up roots in nine days, leaving me to sort it all out.

"He's perfect for me, Dayle," she says. "I can't wait to spend the rest of my life with him."

"You're sure of that?" I am razzing her a little now. It beats crying. "Lifetime commitments are not for wimps, you know. Only the strongest of hearts survive."

"I know that," she says, as if she could.

But does she? Does she know that marriage is a life-altering experience? That she will no longer be free to come and go as she pleases? That a commitment of this magnitude will sometimes demand she do things *just to please her husband?* Does she understand that?

"Yes, it's a big step," she says, "But I love him. Isn't true love enough?"

I smile. She is in a festive mood, and I have no desire to spoil it by launching into one of my notorious philosophical meanderings. Still, I long to tell her that love cannot be labeled, *true love*, until it is tested.

And love's tests can be as simple as putting down the commode lid—for the umpteenth time—or as weighty as enduring financial setbacks, ill health, a daughter's death, a son's rebellion, a sudden disability.

"We are so much alike, Kent and I," she tells me, carefully placing the word *vow* on the Scrabble board. "I feel I've known him forever."

I wonder if I should tell her those feelings intensify with time. That some day she will observe her husband on a stage and know in an instant if he's nervous, just by the way he shuffles his feet or adjusts his tie. That she can watch him across the room in a crowd and know if the smile on his face is genuine or fake. I want her to know that one day she will be able to look into his eyes and hear words he does not speak.

"Can you believe, we've not had one argument?" Amy tells me.

I believe it. A woman of humility and meekness, I cannot imagine my friend arguing with anyone for very long, except me, perhaps. And yet, I want her to know that arguments are OK. Marriage often requires unpleasant negotiations, give and take from both parties.

I feel I should also warn her there may be days when she stares angrily across the table at her beloved, her heart a block of ice. Even so, I'd like her to know there's no need to panic. Love's flame has a remarkable way of melting the coldest of hearts.

"You know we're going to be traveling full time," she reminds me. "I am so excited about getting to travel."

"I'll be expecting a postcard from every historical monument," I tell her, picturing her and Kent driving across bumpy two-lane highways, and wide expressways, holding hands across the console.

I wonder if I should warn her that love's highway can get a bit bumpy as well. Nerve-racking, to say the least. That's when many couples call it quits; too selfish, or too lazy, or too something to push ahead.

Not so with *true love*. *True love* is not a quitter; it's not afraid to cross the rockiest terrain, the hottest deserts, the shakiest of bridges. And should the bridge collapse, *true love* sets out to rebuild it.

Our Scrabble game is coming to an end. For once, I am beating her socks off.

"I miss him already, and we're not even married yet," she says. Kent is off preaching somewhere tonight. "It's like a part of me is missing," Amy tells me.

I want to assure my friend that in marriage, time and space should not be feared. That no matter how far apart she and Kent may travel, whether emotionally or physically, *true love* will bring them back together again.

Later, as I stand on the porch watching Amy get settled into her car, tears spring to my eyes. This is our last night together like this. Our relationship must take on a new face. But deep inside my heart, I wouldn't have it any other way.

I also realize I never answered her question. The one about true love being "enough." Now, I have this sudden urge to shout, "Yes, Amy! True love is enough!" But I don't. I want her to uncover this glorious truth for herself.

In the cold night air, I shiver, my breath making flimsy clouds in the porch light. Amy backs down the driveway, honking her horn as she pulls away. She is smiling and waving. And so am I. For she is about to embark on an incredible journey.

Bon voyage, my dear friend.

"Charity . . . endureth all things."
1 Corinthians 13:7 (NIV)

You devised marriage between a man and a woman, Lord, but You never said it would be easy. Give us the strength to follow love's path till death do us part.

Erasers

I had heard of the "terrible twos." That's why I was pleasantly surprised when my daughter and I breezed through her second year with nary a problem. *Whew!* I thought. *I'm home free.*

All went well until about three months after Anna's third birthday. Suddenly, she became argumentative, ornery, and down-right stubborn. This abrupt change in her personality shocked me. She had always been such a pliant child. How could she change so drastically? And right under my nose. Clearly, I had to get a handle on the situation.

There were days it seemed I did nothing but discipline her. I became so frustrated I phoned my sister one morning, the one who'd already been through the threes.

"Is this normal?"

"Yes," she assured me, "It is perfectly normal."

"What's the secret?" I wanted to know.

"The secret," she told me, "is to keep at it. She has to know you're the boss. When she discovers that behaving in such a way only gets her punished, she'll soon stop."

It sounded simple enough, but it proved difficult to remain firm, to not let some of her smart-aleck remarks go unnoticed. Often it seemed much easier to do tasks myself than to make her obey orders. But I pressed on. I'd seen enough parents who never enforced their rules, and I feared my daughter would become as obnoxious as the children they'd produced.

One day Anna wandered into the bathroom, where I stood brushing my hair. In her hand, she carried a blue ink pen. Using ink pens was not one of her privileges; she had a tendency to write on her legs, not to mention furniture and walls.

"What are you doing with that ink pen?" I asked her.

"Mine!" she said, curtly.

"Well you know you can't use a pen, so let me have it."

She just stood there, staring me down.

"Anna, hand me the pen," I demanded.

But she didn't. Instead she threw it, full force, into the bathroom, where it landed in a sink full of water.

Taking a deep breath, I turned and looked at my daughter, who had an odd expression on her face. "Anna," I said, "that is *not* acceptable behavior in this house, and you know it. I really should march you in there and spank you. Shouldn't I?"

She just stared.

"It makes me sad when you behave like that," I said. "And it makes God sad."

She stared.

"What does Ephesians 6:1 say?" She could quote it, and

I couldn't think of a more appropriate time.

But she only stared.

"It says, 'Children obey your parents,' " I told her firmly. "Now, Anna, I've asked you not to play with pens. Is that obeying me?"

Finally a response. She shook her head.

"And did you obey me when I asked you to *hand* me the pen?"

She shook her head again.

"Well, don't you think you should ask God to forgive you?"

She stared.

"Whenever we do something wrong, we should always ask God to forgive us."

"Why?" she asked.

"Because the Bible says we must *confess* our sins, which means we have to *tell* God our sins. Then He'll forgive us."

She was listening.

"After we tell God our sins, and ask Him to forgive us, then He goes and gets His big eraser and erases that sin off our record. And He never remembers it again." It wasn't exactly Scripture I knew, but it got her attention.

She smiled and straggled out of the room.

Several hours later, I stood fixing dinner when Anna rounded the corner.

"Mother wants you to pick up your toys in the living room," I told her. "Daddy will be home in a little while."

She scooted off, I assumed, to comply. So imagine my surprise when I walked through the living room a few minutes later and discovered the toys unmoved.

"Anna, come here, please."

When she appeared, I gazed at her, my face quizzical. "Didn't Mother tell you to pick up these toys?"

She nodded.

"And didn't I just talk to you about obeying?"

Instantly, she hung her head, closed her eyes. "Sorry, God," she said. "Sorry, Mom." Then, in the meekest voice, with her head still bowed, she asked, "Is it erased yet?"

Yes, Anna. Now and forever!

> *"If we confess our sins, he is faithful and just*
> *to forgive us our sins, and to cleanse us*
> *from all unrighteousness."*
> 1 John 1:9 (KJV)

Father, blot out our transgressions this day.

There will be no song on our lips
if there be no anguish in our hearts.
Karl Barth

A Song in Sorrow

uanita awoke in the night with a strange sensation of fear. It wasn't that she saw or heard anything, but rather, an ominous feeling of impending danger. Perhaps an awareness much like that of an animal sensing the lurking of a devouring enemy, ready to pounce.

For a few moments, she lay in bed, tense, straining to hear something assuring her this was only the vivid imagination of a fourteen-year-old girl. The house was quiet. No one stirred. Her mother, daddy, sisters, and brothers all slept. She felt foolish being afraid like this.

Gradually, Juanita became aware of an odor. A pungent, alien odor so strong it seemed to overpower the air itself. Swiftly, she left her bed and raced to the room where her mother and three-year-old brother slept. "Mama," she whispered hoarsely, "what is wrong?" Rousing from sleep, Juanita's mother assured her she would get up and look around.

Having cast that burden on broader shoulders, Juanita

quickly assumed another one: her baby brother. Such a darling, he lay sleeping soundly. *But how could he be breathing?* Juanita wondered. Her nose stung; she tried not to breathe.

Stumbling to the bathroom, she wet a washcloth in cold water and went back to where her brother slept. Picking up his limp form, she covered his face with the wet cloth and carried him outside to fresh air and safety.

Not until Juanita staggered out the front door, heard the clanging of the fire engines in the damp night air, and watched the red and orange flames leaping high towards the heavens, did she realize her family had fallen victim to a vicious fire. A fire that not only claimed all of their material possessions, but also the life of Baby Sister, as they called her.

Sitting on the ground the next day, under the sprawling, naked branches of a large tree, Juanita and her father viewed the wasted, charred ruins of what once had been their home; their refuge. Her mother and siblings were now in the homes of neighbors and friends. But, for some reason, her dad, in his deep grief, sought the comfort of the outdoors. Juanita wanted to be close to her daddy.

The early November morning was cool, but not unpleasant. Wrapping borrowed clothes around her, Juanita, in her small way, shared her father's sorrow. The yard, that once rang with laughter and joyous shouts of happy children, lay silent, as though paying homage to the beautiful, fair-haired child who would not return there to play. Juanita's father, and the firemen, had done everything possible to save Baby Sister, but her lifeless body was found wedged between a door and the wall.

A Song in Sorrow

With desolation and grief their companions, Juanita and her dad sat there that day, the stillness broken only by the falling of a leaf, or the heavy sigh of the father. Suddenly, from deep within Juanita's soul, came a song. With a voice soft and placid, her song of thanksgiving and praise filled the ashen skies above them.

Turning toward her, Juanita's dad said, in a grief stricken voice, "How can you sing at a time like this?" He looked at her as if she were a stranger.

Honestly, she told him, she did not know. Her music class had been practicing the song for weeks, in commemoration of Thanksgiving. Maybe that was why. Whatever the reason, Juanita kept on singing, her voice growing clear and powerful, surging as water when the floodgates have been removed. The song seemed to cleanse, heal, uplift her desolate spirit. When the song ended, and the last melodious strains settled around her, Juanita's grief had disappeared. The burden of having saved the lives of her family from certain death, the self-imposed guilt of failure because Baby Sister had not made it out, all of those morose feelings vanished. Instead, a sweet sensation of peace enveloped her.

Juanita knows her song came from God that day. And even though she does not consider herself an accomplished singer, she says singing is one thing that has helped carry her through life's trials. "In the difficult times of my life," she says, "when darkness surrounds me, when hope seems gone, somehow, God comes and gives me a song; a song of praise and thanksgiving."

"I will sing unto the Lord as long as I live."
Psalm 104:33 (KJV)

**Dear Lord, when we're surrounded
by the ashes of what used to be,
help us look deep inside ourselves
and find a song of thanksgiving
for all that remains.**

A version of this story first appeared in *Vital Christianity*, written by Juanita Wigginton. Used here with permission.

The mother-child relationship is paradoxical and, in a sense, tragic. It requires the most intense love on the mother's side, yet this very love must help the child grow away from the mother to become fully independent.
Erich Fromm

Mom Goes to Camp

Aunt Dayle?" It's the compelling voice of my niece.

"Hi! Leslie. What's up?"

"Aunt Dayle, can Anna please go to camp with me this year?"

Camp? Can Anna go to *camp?* She's not quite nine years old! I am stunned. Who would tell her to brush her teeth? Comb her hair? Change her socks, for goodness sake? How would she ever be able to get her ponytail tight enough without me? And for a whole week?

It is while Leslie waits for my answer that I am mulling this over. Thankfully, mothers have the unique ability to maintain their outward composure, while going completely berserk on the inside.

"Well, I'll need to think about it, Leslie," I say calmly. "And I'll have to ask Uncle Stan what he thinks. So, I'll call you back in a few days. Bye-bye and be sweet."

My husband's response is predictable. "Absolutely not!"

he says. She's too young."

I decide not to mention it to Anna just yet, but as luck would have it a few days later, Leslie calls and just happens to mention the word "camp." That did it.

"Please, Mama," Anna says. "I want to go s-o-o-o-oo bad. Pl-e-e-e-ase?" Her eyes, the color of chocolate drops, plead her case.

The ensuing week centers around the "C" word, and even though Stan and I finally give our consent, I remain uneasy about it.

It is that same uneasiness that rushes over me like a tidal wave as my sister, Gayle, and I drive onto the campground several weeks later.

A sea of youngsters swarm in every direction, looking, for the most part, as I fear Anna will as soon as I am out of sight: hair disheveled; clothes rumpled; shoes untied; hard candy hanging out of their mouths.

Registration moves slowly, but at last the four of us stand inside a sweltering dormitory, staring at rows of metal bunk beds atop bare concrete floors. My stomach lurches at the thought of leaving my child—my *baby*—inside this place for a whole week. I long to grab her in my arms and run.

But one look at her face tells me that would be unwise, for she and Leslie are beaming from ear to ear, standing proudly before the bed they've chosen as "theirs" for the week. Could we please unload their luggage?

Gayle and I exchange terrified glances, but somehow manage to stumble outside and return with our daughters' suitcases, holding fresh-smelling clothes and linens.

As I spread Anna's sheets across the puny mattress, I hear

Gayle imparting motherly advice to Leslie about something or other, so I decide to offer Anna yet another lecture concerning housekeeping and oral hygiene. It is one of many I have delivered since arriving.

"Remember Anna, when you finish showering, you need to hang your washcloth and towel over your bed rail to dry. If you just throw them in a pile you'll come home with mildewed clothes." Her eyes are on my face, but her expression never changes. "And don't forget to brush your teeth and . . . Anna, are you even listening to me?"

"Yes, *ma'am!*" she says, adding an edge to her tone, which I, reluctantly, ignore.

"And comb your hair out at night or it'll be so tangled the next day you can't. OK?"

"Mama," she says, "I know you're worried about me and everything, but . . . Are you finished? Me and Leslie want to go get something to drink. We're about to thirst to death."

Just then, one of the dorm counselors announces that teams are now being formed for a volleyball game, starting in thirty minutes. All interested, please come forward.

Our girls, obviously thrilled, bolt upright from where they sit on the edge of the bottom bunk. Quickly, they are assigned to a team, and now they are quite ready for something to drink.

Again, terrified looks pass between my sister and me. It appears our time of reigning is swiftly passing.

"Okay, girls," Gayle says. "I guess this is goodbye for us."

Anna's smile fades. She looks at me. "But my team is fixing to play, Mommy," she says. "Can't you stay and watch me?"

Upon hearing her call me "Mommy," I am filled with hope. Maybe this is a sign she still needs me. Regardless, how can I refuse to watch her play? Of course I'll stay.

After the game, Gayle and I know we have to be going. It's getting late and a four-hour drive looms ahead of us.

I call Anna over to me. "You played great, baby!" I tell her. But she hardly looks at me. She's too busy observing the horde of kids making a beeline for the cafeteria where dinner is being served.

"Well, I guess Mommy's gonna go, Anna," I tell her. "Are you sure you want to stay?"

"Yes ma'am," she says, wearily. I've only asked her that question a dozen times.

"Then I guess I'll see you on Friday." Secretly, I hope she'll clutch me in one of her best bear hugs. But she merely nods and smiles. I resist the urge to hug her; I wouldn't want to embarrass her. Instead, I kiss the top of her head. "Bye, Angel. I love you."

Watching our daughters sprint toward the dinner line, Gayle and I let out a collective sigh. It is a pitiful sort of sigh, and my heart hurts.

"Let's swing by the dorm again," Gayle suggests, for whatever reason.

Rummaging in Leslie's suitcase, I watch my sister draw out a yellow sheet of notebook paper. From where I stand I see the impressive title: "Important Things." Underneath, she has listed a string of instructions a mile long.

I open my mouth to tell her she has wasted her time— and ink—creating such a list, but then she turns to me and says, "You know, If I had some tape, I could hang this right here above Leslie's bed where she could read it every day."

She's got to be kidding. "Gayle!" I say harshly, startling her. "Put that down and let's get out of here before we end up spending the week!"

Throwing up her hands in surrender, she grabs her purse and, for once, obeys me.

It is while we are walking to the car that I begin laughing, and I cannot stop. Perhaps it is the absurdity of our feeble attempts at last-minute instructions to our daughters who hadn't heard a word we said. Or maybe it's because Gayle's face, as she clutched that yellow sheet of paper, had been so earnest, so hopeful, so . . . *desperate.* But maybe it is because I realize I have just passed another test in the letting-go process of motherhood. Admittedly, it proved painful, but I passed!

As we drive away, I can't resist one final glance toward the dinner line. When I spot them—Leslie and Anna—they are standing side by side, talking about whatever nine-year-olds talk about on such occasions, their little faces anxious and eager. It is almost unbearable to look at them standing there, because I know they will never be this small again, because of the way they are growing up, right in front of my eyes.

I give an interminable honk on the horn. Finally, Leslie sees me. Turning to Anna, she points in my direction. I wave frantically. Timidly, Anna waves back. And, ironically, I am suddenly filled with an intense pride that she is able to stand there—without me.

"God is the strength of my heart."
Psalm 73:26 (KJV)

**Dear Lord, the true test of parenting
is in how well our children survive without us.
Please hold me up during those
agonizing goodbyes.**

We live in the present, we dream of the future,
and we learn eternal truths from the past.
Madame Chiang Kai-shek

The Geometry Lesson

Monday morning found me sitting on the couch watching dawn's fingers smear pink across the sky. It had been an endless night. For the past five hours I had alternated between sitting, pacing, and kneeling, pleading with God to eradicate a troublesome problem I'd wrestled with through the years.

My Bible lay closed in my lap. Odd shaped pieces of paper jutted out from its pages where I had marked dozens of scriptures throughout the night. Scriptures like Isaiah 45:2: "I will go before thee and make the crooked places straight: I will break in pieces the gates of brass, and cut in sunder the bars of iron," and Matthew 21:22: "And all things, whatsoever ye shall ask in prayer, believing, ye shall receive."

Weary with fatigue, I clutched my Bible and knelt on the floor.

"Dear Lord," I prayed, "I know I've bothered you all night. It's morning now, and I have to go to work. I wish I could say I felt better than I did five hours ago, but I don't. Please,

God, give me peace about this situation. Give me something of substance to cling to."

As the week unfolded, I found myself returning often to my Bible. Over and over I'd read the marked passages. Still, my spirit waned.

On Thursday, I sat tutoring a student in geometry. Jason was having trouble grasping the concept of how to complete a proof. Invariably, he would argue with what's referred to as the "given" statement. Today was no different.

Studying the constructed figure, he said, "Those lines don't look parallel."

"But they are," I said.

"How do you know?"

"Jason, it says so in your "given" statement. It's something you can assume to be true."

"But they don't *look* parallel."

"Forget what they look like. Proving the lines parallel is not something you're required to do. All you have to do is accept the fact that they are. You will build your proof, and base your conclusion, on that fact."

Before I went to bed that night, I opened my Bible and reminded the Lord of my "situation." *God, I still feel restless inside. I need a special promise tonight.*

Then it came, as clear as the clanging of a bell. The Lord said, "I've given you many promises. Believe them."

That jolted me to an awareness. I was no different from my geometry student. The truth is, God's Word holds an abundance of promises. I must be willing to accept His promises and believe them, no matter how the circumstances appear.

Just like completing a geometry proof, I will never be

successful if I doubt God's "given." Instead, I must use these promises as a foundation on which to build. That is the only way the problems in my life will ever be solved.

"He [Abraham] staggered not at the promise of God through unbelief; but was strong in faith, giving glory to God; and being fully persuaded that, what he had promised, he was able also to perform."
Romans 4:20-21 (KJV)

**Help me understand, Lord,
that having Your promises is not enough.
I must truly believe them.
Only then can I move forward in faith.**

Kindness is a hard thing to give away.
It keeps coming back to the giver.
Ralph Scott

Happy Returns

It had been a stressful week. Everywhere I turned—at the office, at home, on the street—hands were out, begging for more of my time or money. I did what I could, and often without receiving even a simple Thank you. I was glad the weekend had arrived.

July's glorious skies surrounded us as I drove home from church. Beside me, Anna, then seven, sat as pretty as a picture in her long, flowered dress and white patent shoes. Chestnut curls gathered at the crown of her head and dangled in soft coils above her neck.

My heart smote me as I studied her profile, so pure, so innocent. The last few days seemed to have been spent telling her things like, "Just a minute." "I'm busy." "Please, don't bother me now." Yet she sat there without complaint, holding no grudges.

Not me. Today I was full of complaints, and I deeply resented those who robbed me of my time and talents with no mention of appreciation. Was it just me, or had good manners fallen off the face of the earth?

Anna seemed to sense my mood and remained quiet on the drive home. As we rolled into the driveway, she said, "Since Daddy's at work, we can just have our own private time, can't we, Mama?"

I wasn't sure what she meant, but it sounded good to me. "That'll be great, baby. You can help Mama fix lunch, and then we can have our private time." Through the course of preparing lunch and eating it, however, I totally forgot about the private time Anna had suggested.

Now, I sat in my office brooding about nothing in particular and everything in general. In a minute, Anna joined me, settling straight and tall in the wingback chair beside my desk. She smoothed down her dress and crossed her legs. At once, I remembered the "private" time and wondered if this were an indication that it had begun. I turned and smiled at her, saying nothing.

"Mama," she began, "I just want to tell you how good it is to have you and Daddy."

She didn't wait for a response.

"You and Daddy do so much for me. You buy me clothes and give me food," she said. "You take me to a Christian school and buy me toys, and . . . I have a nice chair like this to sit in." Her lips began quivering. "You just do so *much* for me."

By this time, I, of course, had collected a puddle of tears in my lap. Suddenly, Anna bolted from the chair and flung herself into my arms, our tears mingling. We held each other tight for a very long time.

Finally, she pulled away. "I just wanted to say thank you,"

she said, gazing into my wet eyes. "Thank you, Mama."

I hurt recalling the many times during the week I'd neglected my precious daughter's simple wishes, while rushing to satisfy complex requests from virtual strangers who hardly even noticed.

As I looked into Anna's face, the void I'd felt in my heart because of thoughtless and thankless people disappeared. Here was a seven-year-old child who had, unknowingly, taken their place. It would be enough to last a lifetime.

"Do good, and lend, hoping for nothing again;
and your reward shall be great."
Luke 6:35 (KJV)

Dear Lord, when our kindnesses
go unappreciated,
thank You for rewarding us
in unexpected ways.

Growing spiritually is like tea:
it takes hot water to bring out the best.
Anonymous

Passing the Heat Test

I just don't think I can teach that class another weekend," I growled to my husband one afternoon. "It's getting to be too much for me."

Several months earlier, the superintendent at church had approached me, his shoulders slumped, face weary. "You did say you would like to teach, didn't you?" he asked.

"Yes," I said, eagerly "Have you found a place for me?"

He stared at his shoes. "I do have an opening in one of the second session classes," he said, hesitantly. "If you're still interested. That's first- and second-graders."

"Second session?"

"Right. That would be working with our bus kids."

Bus kids. *Great*, I thought. *Just what I needed. A bunch of degenerate children to try and corral on weekends. As if my life wasn't stressed enough already.*

"They are real sweet kids," he assured me. "You'd have about eight at your table."

Staring into the superintendent's face, he looked so sad

and so needy that I said Yes. Thanking me, he handed me the curriculum and strode off with a lighter step.

Even though I had accepted, I had second-guessed my decision ever since. The children were precious, but they could not sit still or quiet for any length of time, which often left me wondering if anything I said was being heard. I felt my talents could be put to much better use elsewhere.

"I think I'll see if another teaching position is available," I said to my husband.

Stan looked vexed. "Well, I'm not a bit surprised," he said wearily. "You're so good at starting something and bailing out about halfway through. Why don't you just teach the class you've been given?"

Ouch! That hit right where it hurt. The worst part was, it was true. Without question, when the going got tough, I had a tendency to make a mad dash for the door, leaving pieces of myself all over the place and not accomplishing much anywhere.

I decided to drop the issue for now, but before I went to sleep, I said a simple prayer; it was a question, really: "*Lord, what do You want me to do?*"

The weekend arrived. With feet like two concrete blocks, I clopped into the classroom and over to my assigned area, spread the activity sheets around the table. Then I waited for the stampede.

Like a herd of cattle, they came. Children of all sizes, shapes, and colors charged through the doors. Six boys and one girl huddled around my table and chattered aimlessly.

As I began the day's lesson, the children refused to pay attention, even though I begged and pleaded, bordering on bribery. I could tell it was going to be one of those days when I wished I'd stayed home in bed.

About midway through the lesson, Sharla interrupted.

"I'm ready to work the workbook," she announced.

"Pardon me?"

"Ain't it time to do our workbook?"

"You'll work in the workbook after I've finished giving the lesson," I said, not a little perturbed. With a strained voice, I attempted to regain my momentum.

"Stop kicking me!" It was Sharla again, glaring at Eric, who had a most baffled look on his face.

Struggling to hold my composure, I said, "Boys, could I *please* have your attention, and Eric, *please* leave Sharla alone."

Silence reigned.

"Let's finish our story," I said, wishing it were already over. I picked up my lesson book and proceeded to share with them the love of God.

"My daddy says there ain't no God." It was Ricardo. His remark rattled me. "There is a God, Ricardo," I said. "And He loves you very much. People who don't believe in God just haven't met Him." Inwardly, I wanted the day to be over so I could go home and laugh around the dinner table with my family. This was depressing. I checked my watch. Ten more excruciating minutes.

Michael raised his hand. "Yes, Michael, what is it?"

"My mama say she gonna give her kids away if we don't stop fussing so much."

While his statement saddened me, I had to wonder what it had to do with the lesson.

He went on. "My little brother cried his self to sleep, and I couldn't get no sleep 'cause he wouldn't hush." Not knowing anything else to do, I patted Michael's sagging shoulders and felt a terrible ache in my throat.

Were these children hearing a word I said? Did it matter? What good was I to them if all I did was sit here listening to their problems instead of teaching them about God?

I remembered my hurried prayer: *Lord, what do You want me to do?*

I wanted to be a teacher, the kind who presented well-prepared lessons with superb crafts, but this seemed little more than babysitting.

At last, class over, the children filed out to the buses at the curb. On his way out, Michael handed me a crumpled piece of paper and awkwardly embraced me around the waist. He looked at me briefly, his dark face breaking into a smile. "Bye," he said shyly, making a run for the door.

As my husband drove home, I sorted through the papers I'd gathered up at the end of the lesson. Among them was the one Michael had given me. Figuring it was nothing more than his completed activity sheet from the workbook, I opened it with little expectation. But it was not his activity sheet. Instead, he had written me a personal note. Scribbled in a childish way were these words: *teecher I lik talking to you I love you.*

My heart smote me. Maybe these kids needed to talk to *me* as much as I needed to talk to them. I realized I had been selfish in wanting to do all the talking. Still, I was not sure my place was in that classroom.

Lord, I prayed silently, *I don't generally ask for a sign, but if you want me with these kids, please show me. I'm desperate!*

The next week unfolded uneventful until Thursday morning when I returned from the mailbox. I stopped to admire the bed of multi-colored impatiens surrounding one end of the house; they looked so lovely all clustered together, each complementing the other.

Then, I saw something I had only heard about. A few feet away, growing between a brick wall and the concrete sidewalk, was a single pink impatiens, the most beautiful I had ever seen.

So incredible was this sight I ran inside and grabbed a camera. As I focused my lens on the flower, I knew it was God's sign to me; I could almost hear Him pleading: *Bloom where you are! Anyone can flourish in fertile soil, but can you bloom in the middle of hot cement?*

"Endure hardness, as a good soldier of Jesus Christ."
2 Timothy 2:3 (KJV)

**Lord, when we find ourselves
recoiling from unpleasant tasks,
remind us that sometimes You place us
in difficult situations in order to see
what we're made of,
to see how well we handle the heat.**

We shall steer safely through every storm, so long as our heart is right, our intention fervent, our courage steadfast, and our trust fixed on God.
St. Francis de Sales

Storms

In the mid-1800s, Horatio G. Spafford was a wealthy man. Not only did he possess great material wealth, he was a deeply spiritual man and spent much time studying the Bible. He and his wife and five children—four girls and one boy—spent a lot of time with godly men like D. L. Moody. To observers, Horatio Spafford appeared to have an ideal life.

But then tragedy struck. A dark cloud hovered over Spafford and his wife as they watched their only son die from pneumonia.

The months that followed were difficult. Still, life had to move on. The girls needed their mother and father, and the loss of their son only made the girls seem more precious.

By 1871, Horatio had invested heavily in property in Chicago along the Lake Michigan shoreline. He possessed buildings and much land. A large plot of land was donated to D. L. Moody's ministry.

While Horatio gave God thanks for the many things he acquired through the years, the memory of his son's death haunted him and reminded him that the Lord gives and takes away.

On October 8, 1871, the Great Chicago Fire occurred. Horatio's property was caught in the middle of it.

With nothing but sad memories in Chicago, Horatio decided to take his family to England where they would join D. L. Moody's evangelistic campaign. Excitement found its way into their home once again as they prepared to sail to Great Britain.

The day before they were to set sail, a member of the Chicago Zoning Commission stopped by and informed Horatio that they needed him to attend a meeting to be held the next evening. At that time, he needed to provide proof of ownership for his extensive holdings along Lake Michigan. If he chose not to attend, his ownership of the property could not be guaranteed. He could either attend the meeting or lose everything.

Upon hearing this, Mrs. Spafford assumed their trip to England would be canceled, but Horatio insisted his wife and girls go on ahead; he would follow as soon as business matters were in order.

As Horatio bade goodbye to his wife and four daughters, he prayed for their safe sailing and for them to soon be reunited. But the greatest tragedy of Spafford's life was just ahead.

One afternoon, the ship carrying Horatio's family ran into a great fog and was caught in the path of another English vessel. In minutes the ship went down.

While the papers said most of the passengers survived, Horatio had no way of knowing if his family was safe. Finally, a telegram from his wife came with the sad news. It read: "Saved alone." In one day, Horatio had lost all four of his daughters.

He boarded the next available ship to meet his wife in England. While on the ship, he asked his traveling companion to inform him when they reached the approximate site where his daughters had perished. It was then that Spafford went up to the deck of the ship to pray and think about his daughters who had died.

From the depths of his sorrow, Spafford picked up a pen and began to write:

> When peace like a river attendeth my way;
> When sorrows like sea billows roll.
> Whatever my lot, thou hast taught me to say,
> It is well, it is well with my soul.

He cabled the words back to his friend and musician, Paul Phillip Bliss. By the time the Spaffords returned home, Bliss had composed a melody to the poem, which became the beautiful hymn, "It Is Well With My Soul."

Now, more than a hundred years later, this song continues to bring hope and comfort to the brokenhearted and weary Christian.

"If in this life only we have hope in Christ,
we are of all men most miserable."
1 Corinthians 15:19 (KJV)

Storms

No matter what tragedies befall us today, Lord, our future is bright as long as we walk with You.

The book, *101 Hymn Stories*, by Kenneth Osbeck, published by Kregel Publications, Grand Rapids, Michigan., was used as a resource for this story.

God pardons like a mother, who kisses the offense into everlasting forgetfulness.
Henry Ward Beecher

Lost and Found

 can't recall everything about that night, but the sketchy details go like this: Our town was holding its annual "midnight madness" sale. All the merchants would remain open until midnight, which was something to get excited about in the sixties.

Not one to miss a bargain, Mama herded me and my two sisters into the Pontiac, drove into the little town ablaze with lights, streets lined with cars. After circling Main Street a couple of times, Mama parked two blocks away in a dimly-lit corner parking lot. We piled out and headed for the bright lights and big sales.

What happened next remains somewhat ambiguous, except I do remember one of my sisters had just begun experimenting with hairstyles, and this night I felt she had gone a bit overboard with originality. Being the awkward age of twelve when it seems the whole world is staring at you anyway, I feared the sight of my sister's appearance might cause a sidewalk traffic jam. It was for this reason that I lagged behind, hoping nobody would think I had anything to do with the state of my sister's hair. In retrospect, a silly, selfish thing to do, but quite typical of a twelve-year-old seeking independence.

Our shopping spree began in an elegant, two-story department store, filled with delicacies I could only wish for. Out of the corner of my eye, I kept a careful watch on Mama, not wanting to be with her, not sure of being without her.

For a while, I hung out at the cosmetic counter, opening the lipsticks, spraying the perfumes, daydreaming. Mama didn't seem to notice my absence and pretty soon, she disappeared altogether.

Enjoying my new-found freedom, I wandered off down the crowded sidewalks, gazing hungrily into the windows. At the end of the street, I turned and saw a pair of black patent leather pumps sitting in the window of Cinderella's Shoe Store. On impulse, I went in and tried them on. The heel looked higher than anything Mama had ever let me wear. And they were on sale. I loved them instantly. *Maybe Mama will buy them for me tonight*, I thought, and wondered if my family had missed me yet.

I left the shoe store, leaned up against the window, and waited, thinking Mama'd appear soon. It was dark already, but the longer I stood there, the darker it got. Shoppers rushed past me, laughing, clutching noisy paper bags, having a good time. But I wasn't. I felt alone. And afraid. I wished my throat would stop hurting. I wished I hadn't wandered off.

I decided to backtrack to the department store where we'd begun the evening. The closer I got, the faster my pulse raced. Once inside, I searched everywhere.

But they weren't there.

Where were they? How could I have missed them? It had to be nearing eleven o'clock, I figured. Trying not to cry, I headed back to Cinderella's, combing every store in between. No luck. That's when the awful truth set in: I was lost.

Panic hit. Maybe I could find the parking lot and sit it out in the car. They could not go home without the car, I reasoned. Which meant I would, eventually, be found.

But finding the car proved a difficult task for a scared twelve-year-old kid. Was it one block over? Or two? Did we turn left at Main Street? Or right?

In a frenzied state of mind, I bolted into a clothing store and ran wildly down the hardwood aisles, sounding like a herd of buffalo, oblivious to the bewildered stares around me. When I reached the end of the aisle, and without asking, I crashed through the stockroom, climbed over a pile of empty boxes, jerked open the back door marked, "Exit," and found myself in the longest, darkest alley I have ever seen. I'm not sure where I thought I was going.

My heart froze, but the adrenaline pushed me across the narrow alley into another back door marked, "Entrance." Inside, I came face to face with a group of old men seated on stools, smoking cigarettes. I'm sure they were janitors, waiting for the store to close, but this night they looked like ghouls to me.

Petrified, I charged through a divider curtain, ran down the aisle of the store, and plunged out the front door to the sidewalk. I stood there breathless and trembling.

And then I saw it. There, in the dim light of the street

lamp, sat the blue Pontiac, glowing like a beacon in the night.

With great relief, I ran to it and collapsed in tears onto the front seat, wondering how on earth this promising night had ended up such a nightmare.

The town's drunks staggered up and down the street now. Never had I been so frightened as I inched down into the floorboard.

"Oh, God!" I sobbed, "Please let my mother know where to find me . . . *please!*" I thought about screaming, "MA-AA-MA-AA!" to the top of my lungs, but knew she'd never hear me. So, I did the only thing I could think to do.

With quivering arms, I reached up and blew the car horn with all my might. I'd blow a while, and bawl a while. Blow and bawl. Blow and bawl.

After what seemed an eternity, I heard familiar voices approaching. I had been found!

Amidst a barrage of severe where-were-you questions from my sisters, Mama didn't say much. She probably felt like shaking me, but I think she sensed I had already paid dearly for my sin.

As she maneuvered the Pontiac out of the dismal parking lot, I got my nerve up. "How did you know where to find me?" I asked her.

With a rock-solid voice, Mama replied, "I recognized the horn."

Her answer astonished me then, and still does today. In a town brimming with cars and people and noises of the night, Mama heard the feeble sound of a horn—blocks away—and knew it was the desperate cry of her lost child. How? It remains one of the mysteries of motherhood.

Through the years, I've often thought about the lessons I learned that night. First, there is no promised safety away from the flock; it is risky to stray. But I also learned that when I do wander off—and I have, many times—there is One who is listening for my SOS call. It may sound rather ordinary to the casual bystander, but not to Him; He recognizes the cry of each little sheep. And, like Mama, whenever He finds me, He doesn't chide me over and over for my foolish ways.

"The righteous cry out and the Lord hears them;
he delivers them from all their troubles."
Psalm 34:17 (NIV)

Dear Jesus, to be lost is scary.
To be found, divine.
Thank You for finding me.

Live your life and forget your age.
Frank Bering

The Days of Our Lives

It was a pleasant September evening, just weeks before my birthday. My husband and I had gone with our daughter to a local eatery for a late-night snack. For months, my spirits had sagged, anticipating the arrival of this birthday. There was no getting around the truth: Time was flying. Another decade had passed, and I was petrified.

Earlier in the week I had confided to a friend my fears of aging. "It's just a number, Dayle," she had reminded me. "Nothing more."

The number wasn't what bothered me, I told her. It was much more multifaceted. First of all, my body was changing—something, I hate to admit, I had cried about on more than one occasion. This "changing" included strength and stamina, as well as appearance. And then, there was the way society, as a whole, viewed aging women. From my observations, when they weren't patronizing them or mocking them, they ignored them. This only irritated more when I observed that the same treatment didn't seem to hold true for aging men.

And finally, there was the bothersome idea that older women lost their usefulness, that nobody needed them, or even cared what happened to them. I'm not sure how long I'd held that conviction, or even why; without question, most of the positive influences in my life had been older women. Still, this notion had consumed my thoughts in recent months.

As I brooded, our waitress approached and placed glasses of water in front of us. I couldn't help but notice how old she looked. Her gray hair was gathered at the nape of her neck and coiled into a smooth bun. Deep wrinkles spiraled down her face in every direction. The skin on her arms hung loosely below her sleeves.

Straightening up, she smiled and said, "Hello, my name is Betty, and I'll be your waitress tonight. Are you folks ready to order?"

We ordered, Betty took away our menus, and strolled off with a lively motion in her step.

She's probably just faking it, I thought. *She probably hates her job and can't stand to look at herself in a mirror. With that many wrinkles, and that much flab, how else could she feel?*

In a minute, I heard rambunctious laughing coming from behind the counter. Turning, I saw a smooth gray bun moving up and down, in perfect rhythm with the loudest laugh. Betty and a co-worker were trembling, obviously sharing a joke.

Curious by now, I found myself watching Betty's every move. Apparently, some of the counter customers were regulars, because occasionally Betty would call out things like, "You need more coffee over there, Harold?" or "Carolyn, your omelet's coming right up, dear."

Whenever an order appeared in the kitchen window, Betty lost no time in collecting the items onto the large round tray, hoisting it above her right shoulder, and crossing the room in an unswerving manner. I was entranced by the way she rushed around tables carrying steaming dishes and pitchers of iced tea. Quite a pro, Betty.

I especially noticed how she paid extra attention to the children, giving each one a bit of personal conversation, making eye contact, patting a toddler on the head. When my daughter expressed a desire for some pickles with her hamburger, Betty didn't bring just a few pickles, but a bowl full. "There ya go, sweet pea," she said, smiling.

As I watched Betty clearing away dirty dishes from the counter, I heard the cashier call to her. "Betty," she said, "Tom's here." Quickly drying her hands on her apron, Betty rushed to the front of the restaurant where a tall man, about my age, stood dangling car keys.

Betty hugged him, and they stood there making conversation, which I couldn't decipher. In a minute, Tom pointed toward the glass doors. Betty's gaze followed, and she waved and blew kisses, evidently, to someone waiting in a car.

When their conversation concluded, Tom put an arm around Betty's shoulders, gave her a slight hug, then walked toward the door. As he turned to give a final wave, Betty called out, "I love you, son. Drive careful."

When Betty brought our check, I looked into her face more deeply than I had earlier. Instead of the aged body and gray hair, I saw a woman who cared about life; a woman who enjoyed her job; a woman who liked her customers; a woman who loved her son; a woman who, in my opinion, had every reason to frown, yet didn't.

I left the restaurant refreshed. Even though I sensed my fears of aging would return again and again, this night Betty had shown me that getting old does not mean we cease to affect others. This was evidenced by the smile I wore on my face as I settled into the car for the drive home.

"Be strong, and of good courage;
dread not, nor be dismayed."
1 Chronicles 22:13 (KJV)

Lord, the days of my life are in Your hands.
I have no reason to dread.

The first lesson of life is to burn our own smoke;
that is, not to inflict on outsiders our personal
sorrows and petty morbidity, not to keep
thinking of ourselves as exceptional cases.
James Russell Lowell

Danny's Gift

t 5:30 a.m., Sandra Klaus crawled out of bed. It was the Lord's day, as most people called it, but she felt less than hallowed.

"Why must I live like this?" she muttered, snatching her Bible, teaching materials, and pillow. "This is the pits."

Sandra's husband, Ron, was in seminary, and every weekend found them driving 120 miles, one way, to the small church he pastored.

During the two-hour drive, Sandra found herself deep in the pit of discouragement and self-pity. *Life isn't fair*, she thought. *I have to work all week at my job, and on weekends I have to work at Ron's.* She managed to spend a few minutes reviewing her lesson for the children before taking the wheel so Ron could look over his message one final time.

As the car rolled into the graveled drive at the church, Sandra swiped at her hair with a brush and plastered on the smiling face she knew the folks would be expecting.

It was exceptionally hot as Sandra and Ron made their

way into the tiny church. The church had no air condition-ing, which only deepened Sandra's ill feelings.

At the end of the service, Ron and Sandra stood at the front door and greeted church members as they departed. Ron shook each hand and offered an uplifting comment, while Sandra groaned about the intense heat.

In a few minutes, the parking lot emptied. Ron and Sandra collected their things and drove another twenty miles for lunch at a member's home. It would have to be a quick meal, since Ron had to drive yet another thirty miles to lead an afternoon service at a nursing home. On the drive to the nursing home, Sandra prayed the pianist would show up. But she didn't.

"Why are people so undependable!" she growled, know-ing she'd have to struggle through the only three songs she could play. There was no time to brood about it, however. The nursing home residents were now straggling in, some in wheelchairs, some with walkers and canes. Sandra greeted each one with a fixed smile and the same question: "How are you?" She didn't bother to listen to their replies until Danny came in.

Danny, a young man in his early twenties, had been se-verely injured in a car accident some years back. His days were now spent in an adult "high chair" with wheels. With little control of his limbs, Danny was a pitiful sight.

Taking Danny's chair from the nurse, Sandra pushed it to his usual spot in the back row. "There you go, Danny," she said, looking at his face. "Good to see you. How are you?"

His answer was garbled, as usual. Smiling, Sandra nodded and started to walk away, then stopped. She felt drawn to Danny. Perhaps the Lord would have her listen to this young man.

"Not today, Lord," she begged. "We're already running late . . ." But still, she sensed God pleading with her to stay. So, pulling up a chair, Sandra said, "I'm sorry, Danny. I couldn't understand what you said. Try it again."

Struggling to form words correctly, Danny forced out something that sounded like, "Icanoco . . ."

"Try it again," Sandra coaxed.

"Icanoco . . ."

Over and over, Danny tried to say something, but to no avail.

"Let's do one word at a time," Sandra suggested.

Danny started with, "I."

Sandra repeated, "I."

"Ca."

After numerous wrong answers, Sandra said, "Can. I can." This brought a smile. "Now what, Danny?"

Danny emitted an "n" sound, which Sandra quickly interpreted as "not." "Okay. I cannot," she said. "You cannot what, Danny?" Out of the corner of her eye, she could see Ron was impatient, but still she knew had to hear this one out.

Danny labored. Then, almost intelligibly, he said, "Come."

"I cannot come?" Sandra asked.

Danny nodded.

"Of course you can, Danny," she assured him. "Look, you're already here. What do you mean you can't come?

To the service?"

Danny's head waggled from side to side. "No," he said, "I cannot come pla . . ." But then his words were lost again.

"You cannot come play?" Sandra asked, groping for understanding.

No, that wasn't it either. After a while, Sandra realized Danny was merely answering her question, "How are you?" His answer was simple: "I cannot complain."

Suddenly, she understood why the Lord forced her to listen to Danny. She'd spent her entire day complaining, when she had so much to be thankful for.

"Danny's words should have been mine," she says. "Now, when life caves in around me, and I'm tempted to feel sorry for myself, I remember Danny and his message that day: 'I can *not* complain.' "

**"A word fitly spoken is like apples of gold
in pictures of silver."**
Proverbs 25:11 (KJV)

**When we're full of complaints, Lord,
place a Danny in our midst.**

A version of this article appeared in *Home Life*, written by Sandra Klaus. Used here with permission. Copyright 1993 by Sandra Klaus. Sandra is a pastor's wife in Oblong, Illinois, and a writer for Gospel Missionary Union (Kansas City, Missouri).

*Calvary shows how far men will go in sin,
and how far God will go for man's salvation.*
H. C. Trumbull

The Greatest Gift

On Friday, several weeks before Christmas, I crouched on the floor sorting through piles of crumpled sheet music stashed in my piano bench. I had avoided the task way too long. Four-year-old Anna sat beside me. Before long, the rug was piled high with bulging folders of music. Wedding music, hymns, lots of Christmas music.

Suddenly, my hand fell upon a paperback book of Christmas carols. "Oh, look, Anna," I said, handing her the small book. Together, we flipped through its pages, oohing and aahing over the marvelous artwork. Across from each carol, a colorful watercolor painting illustrated the song. Each piece featured small, cherubic children; their simple profiles sent a lump to my throat.

After a while, I left Anna with the book and returned to sorting through the music on the floor. In a minute, I heard a sniffle, and then another sniffle.

Turning, I saw Anna was crying, the little book of Christmas carols crushed tightly against her chest.

What's the matter, sweetie?" I said, surprised.

Meekly, she laid open the book. "This picture, Mama," she said. "I just love this little picture." Her small voice came out in gentle sobs, as she pointed to the song entitled, "What Child Is This?"

There sat Mary, a holy admiration on her face, cradling the most beautiful baby I had ever seen. I stared for a long moment. It was a touching sight, indeed.

Gathering Anna close, I retold the Christmas story, but I didn't stop there. Christmas, I explained, was simply the first step toward Calvary, the place where Jesus took on the sins of the world so we could have salvation.

When I finished talking, Anna's small body trembled as tears ran, unchecked, down her cheeks. Raising her face upward, squeezing her eyes tight, she pressed the cherished picture to her body, and, in a sort of desperate cry, she said, "Oh, God! Thank you so much for Christmas."

Her heartfelt worship overwhelmed me. Clearly, the familiar story of Christmas, the one she'd heard over and over, was not just a story this day; Anna had grasped its message, its purpose.

Taking her tiny hands in mine, we gazed into each other's eyes, great tears spilling onto our cheeks. Hard as I tried, I could not speak. The lump in my throat would not budge. But it mattered little. I knew Anna had said it all.

"And the Word was made flesh,
and dwelt among us . . ."
John 1:14 (KJV)

The Greatest Gift

Almighty God, without a doubt,
the greatest gift ever given
came wrapped in a robe of flesh.
Emmanuel . . . God with us.
Our grateful hearts rejoice.

Nothing is worth more than this day.
Goethe

A Day to Remember

At seven o'clock, Curtis McNatt waved wildly in the general direction of the alarm clock, hoping to quiet its screams. At the same time, five-year-old Michael sat just outside his parents' bedroom door, fully dressed. He had waited forever for this day.

His suitcases were at the back door, along with his baseball bat and glove, one fishing pole, and a tackle box the size of Montana. Michael was ready. He had even brushed his teeth. All he needed was his father to wake up and drive him to Jeffrey's.

Curtis McNatt had been a heart surgeon for seven years now. While he considered his profession a high calling, it did have its drawbacks. He'd watched husbands and wives torn apart by death's unexpected visit. He knew what it meant to look into the faces of a frightened family and tell them their mother needed a new heart. And he also knew he worked too many hours. But it was Friday, and Dr. McNatt had the weekend off, although he could certainly think of better ways to spend it.

With his wife, Marsha, seven months pregnant, it had fallen Curtis's lot to drive a hundred and fifty-two miles north to his sister-in-law's home—in the boonies, as he called it—where he would leave Michael for a week's visit with cousin Jeffrey. They were a wild pair, Jeffrey and Michael, and Curtis was grateful he had to spend only one night under the same roof with this boisterous duo.

"Are you ready, Dad?" Michael inquired, even though, now standing, he could plainly see his dad squirming and moaning into a pillow.

Curtis muttered something about being there in a minute, and that was all Michael needed to hear. He charged into the room, kissed his mom goodbye, bolted down the hall, collected his stuff, placed it in the back seat of the car, and piled in beside it. And that's where he was when his dad strode out fifteen minutes later, looking somewhat strange without his white lab coat and black leather briefcase.

After a quick stop for breakfast at McDonald's, Curtis steered the car in the direction of Highway 47, a two-lane, endless strip of asphalt with nothing but trees and fields on either side. Curtis figured he'd set the cruise on sixty and let her rip. He hoped Michael hadn't forgotten his headphones and tapes; he, Curtis, sure wasn't up to talking for the next couple or so hours.

They'd been riding almost an hour when the red light on the dashboard lit up, indicating the engine was hotter than normal. And when the dash started beeping, Curtis figured he'd better pull over and have a look.

Smoke seeped out the cracks as he popped the lock and

raised the hood. Not mechanically inclined, he hadn't an inkling as to what might be wrong. He'd guess the radiator, but that was just a guess.

Michael dove out of the backseat looking troubled. "Does this mean I can't go see Jeffrey?" He said it as though no greater catastrophe could occur in his lifetime.

"What it means," Curtis said, "is that we definitely have a problem, and no, you may not get to go see Jeffrey."

"But I *need* to go, Dad. Me and Jeffrey have to feed the chickens, and Aunt Nina said Uncle Brian was taking us fishing tomorrow. Jeffrey said so, and Grandpa let me bring his tackle box."

Curtis wasn't listening. He led the grieving Michael back to the car, grabbed his mobile phone, hit some numbers, and waited until a voice answered.

"Yes, this is Dr. Curtis McNatt," he said, hoping the "doctor" would carry weight at the other end of the line. "I'm stranded out here on Highway 47, just north of Junction 288. How soon could I get a wrecker out?" He paused, listening. "Is that the quickest you can be here? Okay, then. Come straight out 47 about fifty miles. You can't miss me; I'm on the right-hand side."

He hung up the phone and turned to Michael who was jamming his fists into his backpack like a boxer. Pow! Pow! Pow!

"Look, son, it'll be at least an hour and a half, maybe more, before the wrecker comes. We may as well go sit in the shade; it's cooler out there than it is in here."

Twigs cracked and snapped as the two weary travelers shuffled to the giant oak and sat down. For a long while, they stared at the car, Michael wishing he was at Jeffrey's, Curtis wishing he'd never agreed to this outing. He turned and gazed at his little son's face, so much like his own. He knew they couldn't sit here staring at the car for ninety minutes, but what was there to talk about?

Outside of the operating room, Curtis often felt like a fish out of water, especially with his son. Maybe he should enroll in a night class at the junior college. Something called "How to Be a Father." Now, he had another one on the way and Marsha would need his hands-on participation more than ever. The thought scared him.

"Dad?"

"Hmm?"

"When is the baby coming?"

The big event was never far from Michael's thoughts.

"About two months, I reckon, son."

"Do you think it might come while we're sitting under this old tree?" He always managed to think of worst-case scenarios.

"Michael, I just said it'd be about two months. I sure hope I'm not sitting under this tree for two whole months."

"Will I already be in school?"

Curtis thought a minute. "Yeah. You'll already be in school. Are you excited about going to kindergarten?"

"Yeah, but who's gonna take me?"

"I guess your mother will."

"But she'll have the baby."

"So. She can still carry you to school; it's only two miles from the house."

"But what if the baby cries so loud and keeps her up all night and she's too tired to get up and take me to school?"

"Son," Curtis was getting irritated, "why are you worried about this? Your mother will take good care of you and see you get to school. Mothers do it all the time." He glanced at his watch. Twenty-one minutes had expired since he'd phoned the wrecker. Twenty-one lousy minutes.

"Dad?"

"Hmm?"

"Why can't *you* take me to school?"

It had never crossed Curtis's mind why he couldn't take his son to school. True, it would be right on his way to the office, but he just figured, well, he just figured he couldn't. Doctors were busy, important people.

"Say, Dad. Why can't *you* take me to school?"

Curtis was used to Marsha bailing him out whenever Michael asked one too many questions. But she was snuggled in bed, he imagined, and he was here sitting beside his son on a lonely stretch of highway, and it was definitely his question to answer. So, he shifted his weight, stalling, and finally sputtered, "I don't know, son. I, uh, I guess, uh, I uh, suppose . . ." He cleared his throat, which suddenly seemed dry as a haystack. "I guess we, uh, might could try that, me taking you to school." He sneaked a quick peek at Michael, who was hugging his knees, his gaze fixed hard on his shoes.

Nobody moved. After a minute, Michael straightened his back, let out a sigh, and said confidently, "That'd be better, don't you think, Dad?"

"What, me taking you to school?"

"Yeah." He waited a few seconds. " 'Cause we're both boys. Aren't we, Dad?"

The smile on Curtis's face was not planned. It just happened.

And neither had he planned to reach his long arm out and pull his little son closer. It just happened. And when it did, the two "boys" looked at each other, and in that split second, Curtis felt something inside his chest he'd experienced only one other time in his life, and that was when Marsha floated down the church aisle on the arm of her father, a vision in white. But it was that same tightening, almost painful feeling in his chest, inching upward, threatening to cut off his very breath.

Later, Curtis stood watching a stranger hook his lifeless car up to a yellow wrecker. At first, it had seemed like an awful thing to happen, the car breaking down, but now he knew it had been a blessing from above. A real blessing from above.

As the trio drove off in the cab of the tow truck, northbound to the Exxon service center, Curtis reached for his mobile phone and punched some numbers. While he waited for his sister-in-law to come on the line, he tousled a five-year-old's pale hair.

Michael would be a little late, he'd tell Nina, but not to worry. He was in good hands. Yes, Michael would certainly be there. After all, he had chickens to feed and a lake full of fish to catch. And just maybe his father would borrow a pole and stay on an extra day.

> *"This is the day which the Lord hath made;*
> *we will rejoice and be glad in it."*
> Psalm 118:24 (KJV)

Father, how many idle hours
have slipped through our hands
because we failed to recognize their value?

If we were half as concerned with the condition of our souls as we are with our outward appearance, we'd have converted entire cities by now.
Anonymous

Shaping Up

taring at myself in the ruthless light that shone on the dressing room mirror, I said aloud, "I look pathetic."

I meant every word of it. While I'd always considered myself a disciplined person when it comes to weight, a good ten pounds had to come off.

In past years, I had lost ten pounds, and I knew exactly how to do it in the kitchen. But this time I wanted to pull out all the stops. I wanted to also be toned and firmed, whatever that entailed. So I felt blessed when I discovered a woman's health club right inside the hospital not far from home.

The first visit included recording my vital statistics, my weight, my body fat percentage, and identifying my goals. I would begin classes—designed to tone and firm my flab—the following week.

Monday found me purchasing tights, socks, leotards, body suits, and sweatbands. I even found a gym bag with coordinating colors. My husband watched with a look that said, *Go ahead, but you'll fizzle out within a month.* Clearly, I deserved that "look." Three years earlier, after my doctor recommended a good exercise program for my back, I had hired a professional trainer to come to my home and devise a customized workout for me. I was ecstatic about the possibilities and did everything she advised—for about six weeks.

Never mind that, I told myself, *this time will be different.*

At one o'clock, Wednesday afternoon, I marched into the gym, my spiffy bag flung across my shoulders in a way I hoped made me appear a veteran at working out.

In the dressing room, I changed into my workout garb, gathered my long hair in a ponytail, took a deep breath to calm my jitters, then joined my cohorts on the exercise floor. I was pleasantly surprised to discover all shapes and sizes represented.

As the music started, a young girl named Kinsey, not weighing more than eighty pounds, stood in front of us and began barking orders.

"Okay! Are we ready?"

I was. At least, I thought I was.

"Stand up nice and tall!" she yelled. "That's it! Let's warm up our shoulders and arms! Here we go! Roll 'em in! Take 'em out! Roll 'em in! And take 'em out! Great!"

Just about the time I mastered rolling 'em in and taking 'em out, the music's tempo shifted, and Kinsey yelled, "Okay! Let's warm up the upper back and those abdominal muscles!"

Oh, boy. I was short of breath already.

"Keep those abdominals tight, ladies! Take it down! And pull it out! Beautiful! Take it down! And pull it out! Great! You feel it stretching?"

Not to worry. The leotard would never be the same.

"Stretch it out!" Kinsey screamed. "Let's use our legs now!"

Mine were trembling violently already.

Kinsey was merciless. "Lunge!" she hollered, in perfect syncopation with the music. "Lunge! Two, three, four. Lunge! Two, three, four. Beautiful!"

Gritting my teeth and trying to appear normal, I saw Kinsey hadn't broken a sweat. To make matters worse, she was staring right at me.

"If you start to feel weak," she yelled, not missing a step of her workout, "take a little break!" She smiled in my direction. "Side to side, now!" she screamed. "Come on, ladies! Push it back! Move those legs! Push it back! Keep that tummy tight!"

A couple of hours later, I dragged into the house and collapsed in a pile on the den floor. So much for the leotard; I wanted my mother. Suddenly, I understood why exercise helped you lose weight: You were too tired to eat.

I still lay in a flaccid heap when Stan arrived home. "What happened to you?" he asked.

"Exercise," I said. "I feel like I've been run over by a truck or something."

"I'll make supper," he offered. I could only groan.

Later, as I trudged to the table, my face a picture of distress, Stan grinned.

"Are you making fun of me?" I asked, annoyed.

"No," he said, chuckling, "I'm not making fun of you."

"Then why are you laughing?"

"I'm laughing at how silly you are."

I looked puzzled.

"There's nothing wrong with your body, Dayle," he said. "And you aren't even close to fat." He patted my shoulder.

As we said grace, our hands clasped as always; I kept my head bowed a moment longer than usual. I wanted to say a special "thanks" for a man who not only knew how to cook but knew how to stay out of hot water as well.

"Bodily exercise profiteth little."
1 Timothy 4:8 (KJV)

Lord, it matters little how toned and firmed
our fleshly bodies may be;
it's our spiritual bodies we need to keep in shape.

Driving Miss Anna

When my husband and I chose to start our daughter in a private school, I wasn't sure we'd made the right decision. Not that I questioned the quality of education—I had friends who'd graduated from this same academy and gone on to earn degrees from respected universities. But my concern was much less weighty.

The school we selected was twelve miles from our home, and, well, that just seemed like an awfully long way to drive a kid to school, especially when you considered making the trek twice a day with hundreds of other suburban commuters. On a good morning, I could drive it in twenty minutes. But those were few and far between; most mornings required thirty-five minutes, one way.

This annoying truth was only magnified whenever I watched the bright yellow school bus stop at the corner in front of my home, pop open its doors, and swallow up the little ones lined along the curb.

How nice, I thought, *just sending your child to the corner to catch a bus. No hassle. Keep on your pajamas and wave 'em off at the front door.*

My complaints about the inconvenience echoed through the house for the first few weeks of kindergarten, but one morning I realized something: No longer did the car merely serve as transportation, it had become a room where I shared my values with my child, where we communicated, mother to daughter, daughter to mother.

During these weekly drives, I caught occasional peeks into my daughter's thoughts. Admittedly, none of our talks proved earthshattering; well maybe to me they did. Her innocent questions and sincere answers revealed plenty about her ideology. At a red light one morning, for instance, she wanted to know what happened to the balloon that had slipped out of her hands into the night air the previous evening. Not just *her* balloon, mind you, but all balloons ever released since the dawn of helium.

I hemmed and hawed, trying not to divulge the end results of escaped balloons to my kindergartner, but before I could finish, she said, with a child's assurance, "I know where them go." She leaned forward, mouth slightly open, eyes peering upward through the windshield. "Them go wa-a-a-ay up yonder and make all the little children happy in heaven."

Balloons were not the only thing Anna wondered about during our weekly drives, and sometimes my answers didn't suffice. When the boys down the street killed a bird, she wanted to know why people killed birds. Some people eat birds, I told her, hoping the necessity of eating would rationalize the boys' mischievous deed.

"Well, they shouldn't!" she said, horrified. "Little birds were not meant to be food!"

"Oh, really? Well exactly what were little birds meant to do on this earth?" I asked her lightly.

Looking me square in the eye, she proclaimed, "Little birds were meant to *sing* to us every morning," as if I were the biggest nincompoop she'd ever met.

Not only did I discover the "purpose" of birds that year, I was also informed that trees were meant to "grow" and should never be "chomped down."

I argued. Without trees, I told her, we'd have no pianos and guitars and wood furniture, no log cabins, no pencils and paper. To no avail. Anna embraced her opinion, and that was that.

Often during our weekly trips, Anna exposed my faults. After being wronged by a friend, I muttered about the challenge of forgiving. "If you don't forgive him," she warned me, "God won't forgive you. And that means you go to jail."

Jail?

My character flaws turned up during other trips to and from school. When her great-grandfather sponsored her in a "fun run," I wondered aloud how to tell him that Anna had been sick, that the school had assigned a substitute "runner" for her. Would he, at almost ninety years old, understand that his $20.00 donation remained in Anna's name, even though she didn't get to run? "Why don't we just tell Granddaddy that everybody had a good time?" I suggested, seeking simplicity. Her little face appeared thoughtful for a moment. "But Mama," she said, "that's skipping words."

In second grade, we bought Anna an aquarium. She picked out three tropical fish for it and named them, Special, Colorful, and Beautiful. Two days later, Special was dead. I was stunned by Anna's devastation. One morning, shortly after Special's "funeral," we drove to school, a solemn pair. She wanted to know why fish die. I tried to tell her that death is a part of life, that sooner or later, everything, and everybody, dies. She said it's not fair. I said life is seldom fair. She cried all the way to school.

There were days Anna fascinated me with her unraveling of nature's mysteries. I remember one cold afternoon, heading home amidst torrential rains when, without warning, a bolt of lightening exploded in jagged fingers across the dark sky. I recoiled, as if struck.

"Don't be scared of lightning," Anna said, reassuringly. "That's just God's hand telling us He loves us, Mama."

By fourth grade, I began noticing changes in our conversations. While she still considered it a crime to cut down a tree and she felt certain that folks who ate little birds were heartless, our talks to and from school often included less noble matters. There were afternoons she bounded into the car chattering about the "awesome" guy in high school (who's way too old for her), or the boy—the one her age—who likes her but is "gross" because he "shows his food when he eats." But the thing I noticed more than anything else was how consumed she was with her appearance. Her hair had to be styled just so or she pouted all the way to school, and when I questioned her about why she stopped wearing a certain pair of socks, she informed me they made her legs look "weird."

Anna's ten now and in fifth grade. Between her father and me, we've logged more than 17,000 miles to and from school, spent more than 700 hours riding side by side. Sometimes we aren't in the mood for talking. There are those days we simply hold hands across the seat. But even during our quietest drives, we always say at least three words: "I love you."

I don't know if Anna will always be as open with me as she is now, but I can hope. For I do know the next few years hold enormous changes for both of us. She will experience what's known as puberty, her body's way of preparing her for adulthood. No doubt, she'll need someone to talk with in private about personal matters. And me, well I'll have my own aging body to deal with, as well as trying to accept hers. Maybe she'll offer valuable insights on such grave subjects. If nothing else, maybe she'll at least hold my hand.

Maybe, if I'm lucky, she will recognize our weekly trips as rare windows of opportunity: she and her mother together, talking, listening, learning. Maybe someday she will know—just as you do by now—how meaningful these, once dreaded, trips have become to me.

"He that has a wise child shall rejoice in him."
Proverbs 23:24 (NIV)

Children are remarkable, Lord.
Thanks for sending me a jewel.

No day has ever failed me quite—
Before the grayest day is done, I come upon some
misty bloom or a late line of crimson sun.
Grace Noll Crowell

A Glimpse of Hope

t one o'clock I locked the door to the crisis pregnancy center, my spirit despondent. Another Wednesday morning had come and gone. I'd counseled only two girls all morning—one eighteen, the other, nineteen—and they both were convinced an abortion was the only viable solution to their "problem." While I'd done the best I could to present other options, I feared, in the end, my words had fallen on deaf ears.

Trudging down the stairs and out to my car, I wondered how it had happened. How had life become so devalued? How could *anyone*, let alone a woman, watch a twelve-minute film showing the development and exquisite features of a ten-week-old fetus, see its beating heart, its ten tiny toes, and remain unmoved?

Breathing a prayer for the girls, and for my fellow volunteers, I drove home more dedicated to the cause than ever.

I awoke earlier than usual the next morning. My sleep had been pierced with haunting dreams. In one dream, a row of small children sat in a semi-circle in front of me. Each of them had a coloring book and a fistful of bright crayons. As they colored, the smiles on their tiny faces turned to giggles, those wonderful belly laughs only a baby can produce. But then, a white smoke filled the room, and when I looked back, all that remained were open coloring books and scattered crayons; the chairs were empty. And silent.

With an incredible ache in my chest, I dressed for work. In the car, I flipped the radio on for company. *Maybe the music will take my mind off my dream*, I thought. But instead of a song, I heard the day's headline news: A newborn girl, found in a box on the hood of a pickup truck in a neighboring city, was recovering in a county hospital. According to officials, the seven-pound baby had been abandoned two to twelve hours after birth. She was wrapped in blankets, and a bottle of formula lay beside her. The hospital staff had named her, Precious.

A trickle of tears slid down my face. What a dismal picture of society. Yesterday life was of no value *before* birth; today, it seemed to have no value after birth.

With a voice void of hope, I looked up into the gray skies in front of me and said, "God, surely there is some good left in this world. Could you please help me find some good today? I am so tired of this world's evils . . ."

So intent was my pleading, I had to suddenly brake to keep from hitting the car in front of me. *Now why is this guy stopping all of a sudden?* I wondered.

And then, I saw it. Up ahead, a big, yellow school bus sat, red lights flashing, waiting for a passenger to board.

In a minute, the traffic inched forward and there, on the

side of the road behind a white picket fence, stood a small, fair-haired woman waving toward the yellow bus, her eyes full of love, her tummy enlarged with the promise of a new life.

Talk about a quick answer to prayer!

I felt mysteriously drawn to the woman at the fence. So powerful was this feeling, I slowed my car to a crawl, rolled down the passenger window, and waited until her eyes met mine. And that's when I waved and shouted across the ditch, "God bless you!" Perhaps she thought I was nuts, but I didn't care.

As I drove away, I watched the woman turn down the narrow lane and move slowly toward her home, morning's mist at her back. I knew the image of her there would sustain me in the days to come.

"Be of good courage,
and he shall strengthen your heart,
all ye that hope in the Lord."
Psalm 31:24 (KJV)

Father, when I am tempted to give up the fight,
let my eyes and thoughts focus
on the good scattered around me.

Every man's life is a plan of God.
Horace Bushnell

Detours

here are we going?"

My husband lay sprawled on the floor, flipping through a large travel atlas. He's had a love affair with maps for as long as I've known him.

He scratched his head. "I was thinking about the Smoky Mountains. How does that sound?"

"Hey," I said, "just tell me when to pack." Then I frowned. "You think the van will make the trip?"

Even though we owned two vehicles, the van was our choice for long trips. It gave Anna and Princess—our large collie—ample room for roaming, and it had a trailer hitch, which we needed for pulling our little camper. The bad news was the van had been in our family since it rolled off the showroom floor in 1983. By this time, it had logged more than 200,000 miles. I feared it might be ready to retire.

"I think it'll make it," Stan said, not sounding as confident as I had hoped.

Six months later, on a brilliant Sunday morning, we rolled along the interstate, looking forward to spending our first official night of vacation in Chattanooga.

"Dad?" It was Anna, from the back of the van. "How many more miles?"

No answer.

"Dad! How many more miles?"

Still, no answer.

"Stan," I said, "Anna wants to know how much farther to Chattanooga." I glanced at my husband, who was staring into the left rear-view mirror, a perplexed look on his face.

"Stan," I repeated, louder. "Are you listening?"

"Yeah," he said, still staring out the window. "I'm listening." He turned to me. "Do you smell something?"

The tone of the question unsettled me. I sniffed. "What does it smell like?"

"Something burning," he said.

I sniffed again. "What do you think it is?"

"I'm afraid we've got a serious problem," was all he said, sending a parade of groans from my lips.

At the next rest area, Stan assessed the situation. Oil was splattered across the back of the van and the front of the camper. It looked ugly, and I felt sick.

Digging out his tools and jack, my husband set out to diagnose the problem while I spread a quilt on the thick green grass, under a giant oak and sank down with my misery.

"It's always something, Lord," I said, gazing up at lush foliage under a sky dotted with plump, fluffy clouds. "Always something." I hugged my knees to my chest, seeking comfort.

In a while, Stan came over and broke the news. There was an oil leak, he said, but he couldn't tell where it was coming from. The next town was only a few miles up the road. If we stopped every few miles and added oil, we should do okay. We'd spend the night there, have the van looked at tomorrow.

Back in the van, we crept along the freeway in silence. Soon darkness gathered at the windows, chasing us into a tidy campground, a place I'd never heard of before: Noccalula Falls, near Gadsden, Alabama. We arrived at our campsite in a dreary mood, set up camp, and fell into bed, exhausted.

In the morning I rose to the inviting odor of breakfast cooking. Through the canvas I could see my husband flipping pancakes in a skillet, four round eggs beside him, waiting to be cracked and scrambled.

Crawling out of bed, I opened the door a narrow crack. "Whatcha doing?"

He smiled. "I'm making the best of a bad situation," he said. "Let's eat!"

Over breakfast, Stan handed me a couple of brochures. "I got these from the office," he said. "Looks like a pretty neat place. I'll take the van in and see what the problem is. I may be gone most of the day," he warned. "Maybe we can go do something tomorrow."

Stan finished eating, drove off at a snail's pace, my prayers going with him. I glanced at the brochures he'd left. *How*, I wondered, *could he always take things in stride?* He was actually expecting to *enjoy* our little visit to this off-the-beaten-path town.

True to his prediction, my husband drove back into camp—in a rented car—just before dusk. From the way he clumped into the camper, I knew it was bad news.

And it was. A full day was needed to repair the van. The estimate was $600.00.

I sat speechless while Stan presented options. "I know that's a lot of money," he said. "If you want to, we can have the van fixed and go home."

This brought cries of distress from Anna, and I wanted this trip as much as anyone. In the end, we decided to "bite the bullet" and go on as planned. Still, I went to bed wondering if this trip was a big mistake.

On Tuesday, we set out on a sightseeing excursion, trying not to think about why we were here. We discovered that Noccalula Falls, lying at the foot of the Appalachian Mountains, is a beautiful place.

Not far from camp, a graveled path wound around to a stone monument of Noccalula, an Indian princess, poised as if ready to jump from a ninety-foot cliff. The ice-cold, clear water below was fed from a slim waterfall, rushing around the feet of Noccalula. Legend has it that this Indian maiden jumped to her death after her father, seeking peace, promised her hand in marriage to the leader of an enemy tribe.

A few feet away, steep, narrow steps, led down into the gorge below the falls. As we crept along the slippery, rocky trail, I paused in a clearing and gazed up at the magnificent falls above me.

Out of the frothy spray of the waterfall, giant cedars

and evergreens rose, and overhead, sunlight broke through a vast awning of branches. Stan turned to me. "It's beautiful, isn't it?" he said.

"Yes," I said. "It's absolutely gorgeous."

At supper that evening, I thought about the enjoyable day we'd spent, and I realized we would never have seen this quaint little place had our trip stayed on course.

I also thought about how quick we are to map out our spiritual journeys, down to the smallest detail. Sometimes we encounter detours along the way. Often we feel frustrated, certain the enemy is "out to get us."

But I'm convinced these detours, no matter how calamitous, are part of God's master plan. We can either turn around feeling defeated, or trust Him to lead us to unforeseen places of beauty; to slow us down and teach us things we'd never learn at our normal breakneck speed.

"Consider it pure joy, my brothers, whenever you face trials of many kinds, because you know that the testing of your faith develops perseverance. Perseverance must finish its work so that you may be mature and complete, not lacking anything."
James 1:3-4 (NIV)

Dear Lord, when we're forced off the beaten path by unexpected woes, help us not be irritated. For not only do You walk with us, You also go before us, preparing the way. Give us the courage to follow wherever You lead.

Epilogue

ou may find yourself surrounded by dark clouds, searching desperately for your "silver lining." Sometimes a silver lining is not readily apparent; I've been there. Others will only be seen in eternity's light. That's why I've included this list of a few of life's treasures. Many of these are my own choices, others I've borrowed from a number of sources. It's my desire that we learn to count our many blessings, regardless of our predicaments.

1. A baby's laugh.
2. Autumn's first breeze.
3. A vase of fresh flowers.
4. Best friends.
5. Playful puppies.
6. A mother's love.
7. A father's love.
8. Newly mown grass.
9. Snugly quilts.

10. Biscuits made from scratch.
11. A child's trust.
12. Music.
13. Vegetables from the garden.
14. Ice-cold lemonade in July.
15. Hot cocoa in January.
16. A day off work.
17. Camping out.
18. Clean sheets.
19. Old dogs.
20. Double-dip ice-cream cones.
21. Vacations.
22. Curious cats.
23. Photographs of loved ones.
24. Grandmother's hug.
25. Grandfather's hug.
26. A surprise party.
27. Winter's first snow.
28. April showers.
29. Manicured flower beds.
30. Little League baseball.
31. Birds singing.
32. A spouse's love.
33. Bedtime stories.
34. A picnic in the park.
35. Seashells.
36. A friendly smile.
37. Helping hands.
38. Clever teachers.
39. Loving brothers and sisters.

40. Concerned pastors.
41. Good neighbors.
42. Doctors who care.
43. Puffy clouds in a blue sky.
44. Sunshiny days.
45. Majestic mountains.
46. White sandy beaches.
47. Lightning bugs.
48. Children playing hide-and-seek.
49. Newborn babies.
50. God's eternal love.